BILLY ROCHE

THE WEXFORD TRILOGY

A Handful of Stars
Poor Beast in the Rain
Belfry

NICK HERN BOOKS

London

A Nick Hern Book

The Wexford Trilogy first published in 1992 as an original paperback
by Nick Hern Books.
This edition first published in 1993 by Nick Hern Books Limited,
14 Larden Road, London W3 7ST.

Cover photos by Richard Blanshard

Set in Baskerville by 🅰 Tek Art Ltd
Printed by Cox and Wyman Ltd Reading

British Library Cataloguing in Publication Data
A catalogue record for this book is available from the British
Library

ISBN 1 85459 265 3

A HANDFUL
OF STARS

A Handful of Stars was produced for television by Initial Film and Television and first screened on BBC-2 in summer 1993 as part of *The Wexford Trilogy*. The cast was as follows:

PADDY	Shay Gorman
CONWAY	Des McAleer
STAPLER	Liam Cunningham
LINDA	Dervla Kirwan
TONY	Aidan Gillen
JIMMY	Gary Lydon
SWAN	Michael O'Hagan

Directed by Stuart Burge, produced by Emma Burge and designed by Christine Edzard at the Sands Films studios in Rotherhithe.

A Handful of Stars was first performed in London at the Bush Theatre on 15 February 1988 with the following cast:

PADDY	Joseph Brady
CONWAY	Peter Caffrey
STAPLER	Breffni McKenna
LINDA	Dervla Kirwan
TONY	Aidan Gillen
JIMMY	Gary Lydon
SWAN	Michael O'Hagan

Directed by Robin Lefevre
Designed by Gordon Stewart & Andrew Wood
Lighting by Paul Denby
Sound by Louise Bates
Artistic Directors for the Bush Theatre Jenny Topper & Nicky Pallot.

Characters

JIMMY, A good looking, tough boy of seventeen or so.
TONY, Jimmy's sidekick. A shy, gauche lad.
CONWAY, A big-mouthed know-all of about thirty-three or four who acts older than his years.
PADDY, An old man who is the caretaker of the club.
STAPLER, A strong, lively man of thirty-three or four.
LINDA, An attractive girl of seventeen or so.
SWAN, A wily detective.

The Setting

The play is set in a scruffy pool hall. There is a pool table, a jukebox, a pot-bellied stove and a one-armed bandit. There are three doors – one leading to the street, one to the toilet and the other leads into the back room where the older, privileged members go. Entrance to the back room is slightly elevated and there is a glass panel in the door through which the caretaker can keep an eye out over his domain. Along one wall there is a long bench and a blackboard and a cue stand and all the usual paraphernalia that can be found in a club of this sort.

The story takes place in a small town somewhere in Ireland. The First Act has a time span of about two weeks. The Second Act takes place the following month, in the course of one night.

ACT ONE

Scene One

The Club with PADDY *opening up the awkward window shutters. When this is done he gets some cue chalk from an old wooden box perched on the ledge and lays three or four squares along the pool table, evenly spaced apart. Then he gets a bottle of Dettol from the cardboard box under the seat and begins sprinkling it around the place, going in through the toilet door to sprinkle some in there, flushing the toilet, coming back coughing, tossing the empty bottle into the waste paper basket. Now he stands and takes a good look at the place, raising up his peaked cap with his thumb and scratching his head. We hear someone knocking on the door and shouting out* PADDY's *name. When* PADDY *does eventually open the front door* JIMMY *and* TONY *come rushing in, both of them trying to make it first to the pool table, nearly knocking poor* PADDY *down in the rush.*

PADDY (*annoyed*). Mind up there the hell out of that. (*He sees the two boys tugging for the best cue.*) Hey cut out the trickactin' there now.

TONY *gives up the struggle and settles for the bad cue.*

JIMMY (*putting in the money*). What kept yeh Paddy? We thought you were after goin' on strike. Set 'em up there Tony. Were you at the pictures or what Paddy? Heads or harps?

PADDY (*still going about his business, doing little jobs*). Yeah. I went up as far as the first house.

TONY. I'm breakin' Jimmy. You broke last night.

JIMMY. Heads or harps?

TONY. Heads.

JIMMY (*tosses the coin onto the back of his hand*). Hard luck. Ha ha ha . . . set 'em up. Was it any use Paddy?

PADDY (*standing on the chair to turn on the outside lights*). Naw.

JIMMY (*chalking his cue*). Hey Tony straighten 'em up there a bit will yeh? *Now* you're learnin'. Come out of me way now.

JIMMY *belts the ball into the bunch a little too aggressively for* PADDY's *liking.*

PADDY. Hey boy, be careful there.

JIMMY. What's wrong with yeh Paddy?

PADDY. That's a brand new cloth on that table. Tear it and it'll cost yeh.

JIMMY. Will you go away and don't be annoyin' yourself Paddy.

PADDY *stops in his tracks and throws the boy a dirty look.* JIMMY *doesn't even bother to respond.* PADDY *goes across to the door leading into the back room and pulls the keys out of his pocket. When he opens up the door* TONY's *head whips around.* PADDY *goes inside and* TONY *rambles over to take a peep in at the room.* PADDY *closes the door over in his face.* JIMMY, *spying that* TONY *is miles away, tries to steal an extra shot.*

TONY. Hey Jimmy it's my shot. What are you wantin', them all or somethin'?

JIMMY. My go. I just potted a ball didn't I?

TONY. Where?

JIMMY (*chancing his arm*). Look come out of me way will yeh.

TONY. You did in me shit pot a ball. Go away yeh chancer.

JIMMY (*conceding*). Alright then, go on.

TONY. I'm not coddin' yeh boy you're the biggest chancer I ever met. I'm goin' to keep an eye on you in future. How am I supposed to play with this auld yoke anyway?

JIMMY. Look stop whingein' and fire.

TONY. I don't see why I should always end up with the bad cue.

PADDY *comes out of the back room carrying a toilet roll.* JIMMY *has played a record on the jukebox.* PADDY *winces, puts the toilet roll on the ledge and goes across to plug out the jukebox. It stops with a jerk.*

JIMMY. Hey Paddy, what's goin' on?

PADDY (*climbing from his knees*). You know well enough that you're not allowed to play the jukebox after half eight.

JIMMY. But sure yeh weren't here Paddy, were yeh?

PADDY. Yeh know the rules.

JIMMY. But sure how am I supposed to play the jukebox if the place is not open?

PADDY *ignores him as he wonders where it was he put the toilet roll.*

Alright then Paddy just give us me money back and we'll say no more.

PADDY *throws him a dirty look.* PADDY *finds the toilet roll and heads towards the toilet.* JIMMY *imitates his walk, making* TONY *splutter and miscue the ball.* JIMMY *spots it and pounces on the chance.*

Hey Tony that counts as a shot.

TONY. Aw no you made me laugh that time. (*Trying to hold* JIMMY *at bay.*)

JIMMY. Come out of it Tony and stop actin' the cannatt. Hey Paddy this lad is cheatin' out here.

TONY. No, fair is fair Jimmy, you made me laugh that time.

JIMMY. That's your hard luck Tony. Come out of it.

The two boys have a tugging match over the table with JIMMY *shoving* TONY *and* TONY *holding on to the edge of the table for dear life.* *Enter* STAPLER, *carrying a handy black bag over his shoulder.*

TONY (*panting*). How's it goin' Stapler?

STAPLER. How's the men? Actin' the bollocks again are yeh?

JIMMY (*giving up the struggle, much to* TONY's *surprise*). Hey Stapler I heard you're goin' back into the ring again.

STAPLER. Oh yes. Old Twinkle Toes is back.

JIMMY. Any fights lined up?

STAPLER. Yeah. I'm fightin' young Harpur tomorrow night sure.

JIMMY. Who? Eddie Harpur? He's good, boy.

STAPLER. He is. He's a good chap alright.

TONY. He'll be no match for our Stapler though.

STAPLER *starts to skip on the spot and begins to shadow box,* *accelerating into a frenzy of rapid punches and blinding combinations.* *He has a dead serious expression on his face and his eyes seem to be* *staring into the eyes of the ghost of his opponent – dancing around after* *him, pushing him into the corner etc.*

JIMMY. Oon the Stapler, you're kickin' the laird out of him now alright.

STAPLER *lets his arms dangle as if the fight is over and looks across at the boys for approval.*

TONY (*standing over the floored body of the make-believe opponent*). You knocked him as dead as a cock, Stapler.

STAPLER. What are yeh lookin' down there for Tony? Up there he is. Hey Paddy, scrape that lad off the ceilin' there will yeh.

PADDY, *coming from the toilet doorway throws his eyes to heaven, shivers with the cold and goes across to the stove.*

JIMMY. Oon Stapler me boy. What do yeh think of him Paddy?

PADDY *sighs and throws his eyes to heaven.*

STAPLER. You can't keep a good man down, ain't that right Paddy?

PADDY (*sighs and mumbles*). Huh you'll get sense so yeh will. Thirty-three years of age . . .

STAPLER (*a little embarrassed*). Were any of yeh at the pictures?

JIMMY. Paddy was.

STAPLER. Any use Paddy?

PADDY (*kneeling beside the stove*). Naw. Bloody hopeless. That's cold. What's wrong with that now I wonder.

STAPLER. I'm surprised at that then. That Robert Ryan is usually good. I love him actin'.

TONY. Yeah, he's a queer smily fecker ain't he?

STAPLER. What? Oh yeah he's kind of sleazy lookin' alright. Good though.

JIMMY. I think we saw that picture before, Tony.

TONY. No, I never saw that one.

JIMMY. I'm nearly sure we did. Hey Paddy, is your man all dressed in black?

PADDY. Yeah.

JIMMY. And does he ride a deadly white horse?

PADDY. Yeah.

JIMMY. Yeah we saw that one alright Tony. Do you remember? He gets shot right between the eyes in the end.

TONY. Don't tell me. I'm wantin' to go and see it tomorrow night.

JIMMY. Sure I'm tellin' yeah we saw it before. Does your man get killed in the end Paddy?

PADDY (*still tinkering with the damper of the stove*). Yeah. The girl shoots him right between the eyes in the end.

TONY *throws his eyes to heaven in disbelief.*

STAPLER (*moving towards the back room*). None of the lads down yet Paddy?

PADDY. No. That's it now. (*He stands up, holding his aching back.*)

STAPLER. Aw sure they won't be long now I suppose. I'll set up the table for a game.

TONY. Do you want a hand Stapler?

PADDY *looks at the boy in amazement.*

STAPLER (*falters*). Mmn . . . Aw no it's alright Tony. Is the special cue closet open or closed Paddy?

PADDY. It's closed. I'll be in there in a minute.

STAPLER. Right.

JIMMY. Hey lads I think we should organise a bus load of supporters to go down and cheer Stapler on tomorrow night. What do you think Paddy?

STAPLER (*from the doorway*). But sure it's only down the road in the Foresters Hall.

JIMMY. Yeah, but it'd look more impressive if we all arrived in a big bus, yeh know what I mean?

PADDY *shakes his head and sighs as he waddles into the back room with* JIMMY *sniggering behind his back.*

Paddy could pay for it out of the funds.

TONY. Do yeh think you'll win Stapler?

STAPLER *shrugs.*

Here come on Stapler, I'll give yeh three round now.

TONY *puts up his guard and shuffles towards* STAPLER.

STAPLER (*letting fly a punch that slaps* TONY *right in the face*). Keep that guard up boy. Watch that . . . and that . . .

STAPLER *has landed a combination of punches that mesmerise* TONY. *Now the two of them dance about on their toes with* TONY *trying to land a punch or two on* STAPLER *who ducks and weaves skilfully. When* TONY *sees the earnest face on* STAPLER *he cowers away from him and* STAPLER *follows him. Finally* TONY *turns and flees around the pool table.* STAPLER *grins fondly at this sight, his fondness for the boy showing in his smile.*

What do yeh think of him Jimmy?

JIMMY. I'm goin' to tell yeh one thing, if he don't hurry up and take his shot I'll be givin' him the greatest kick up the hole he ever got.

TONY (*taking aim*). But sure how could yeh play with this yoke Stapler? Look at the state of it? (*He holds up the cue.*)

JIMMY. A bad workman always blames his tools.

STAPLER (*stepping forward*). Show, give us a look. Sure you'd never learn to play properly with that yoke. Why can't yeh share the decent cue anyway? I mean it's not that hard to pass it back and forward to one another or anything.

TONY. Yeah come on Jimmy, act the white man.

JIMMY (*reluctantly handing the cue across*). Oh here, before yeh burst a blood vessel or somethin'.

STAPLER. That's it. Now you're learnin'.

TONY *bends to take his shot.* STAPLER *goes across and takes a large bottle of lemonade from his bag. He opens it and takes a gulp, belches and offers* JIMMY *a slug.*

JIMMY (*wiping the top of the bottle before taking a slug*). Hey Stapler do auld Matt still be down in the boxin' club?

STAPLER. Matt. Yeah. Sure Matt is the boss. How come I don't see any of you two down there no more?

JIMMY. Sure Matt put me out of the club. The last night I was down there he made me spar against your man whatshisname . . . Healy. He went to town on me I'm not coddin' yeh boy. Didn't he Tony?

TONY. What?

JIMMY. I say your man Healy went to town on me. He bet the head off me Stapler I swear. I wouldn't mind but I hadn't been trainin' nor nothin' yeh know. So I waited outside for him after and I bursted him.

STAPLER. You're not supposed to box outside the ring Jimmy.

JIMMY. Who said anythin' about boxin'. I gave him a headbutt. End of story. I gave him a right furt for himself too I don't mind tellin' yeh. Didn't I Tony?

TONY. Yeah, a royal furt up the rectum.

JIMMY. Wrecked him, I nearly friggin' killed him.

STAPLER. Were you put out of the club too Tony?

TONY. No I wasn't . . . Ah I wouldn't be bothered with that auld lark at all Stapler. Gettin' the head bet off me for a lousy medal.

STAPLER. Mmn . . . I suppose.

STAPLER *looks at* TONY *who is a little embarrassed and afraid that he may have offended* STAPLER's *feelings. Then* STAPLER *glances towards* JIMMY, *a slight hint of condemnation in his eyes.* JIMMY *couldn't care less.* STAPLER *lowers the rest of the lemonade and tosses the bottle into the basket. Then he circles the table, watching* TONY *playing as he walks.*

Keep your chin down Tony. That's it. Good shot. Where are yeh goin' now? Take a good look at the table before you go rushin' around the place. Use your head . . . Hit it low down now . . .

JIMMY. Hey Stapler, let him play his own game.

STAPLER (*ignoring* JIMMY's *words*). Hard luck Tony. Yeh have to use your head Tony. That's what it's all about. Up here for thinkin', down there for dancin'. (*He stands there for a moment to watch* JIMMY *shoot, then he rambles into the back room.*)

TONY. He's queer fast ain't he.

JIMMY *nods that he is fairly fast.*

I'd say he'll beat your man no bother would you?

JIMMY. I don't know. Eddie Harpur is fairly handy.

JIMMY *heads into the toilet just as* CONWAY *comes storming into the club.*

TONY. You're just after missin' it Conway.

CONWAY. What are yeh sayin' feathery feck?

TONY. I said you're just after missin' it here. Stapler is after splatterin' Eddie Harpur all over the place here. I'm not coddin' yeh boy there was blood everywhere.

CONWAY (*unimpressed*). I'd say that.

TONY. I'm goin' to tell yeh one thing boy, he's queer fast.

CONWAY. He'll want to be on skates to get away from that lad tomorrow night.

TONY (*concerned*). Why, would you say he'd beat Stapler?

CONWAY. Are yeh coddin' me or what? Sure that chap is brilliant.

Enter PADDY, *climbing into his overcoat.*

Well Paddy, what did yeh think of that then?

PADDY. Useless. The world's worst now that's all's about it.

CONWAY. The first one wasn't bad.

PADDY. No.

CONWAY. But as for that other yoke. The world's worst is right. I can't stand that Robert Ryan actin' in pictures. (*He sees* PADDY *putting on his scarf which was hanging by the stove.*) Hey Paddy, we're goin' to have a game of poker in a few minutes – as soon as the lads arrive – will you be back or what?

PADDY. Yeah, I'll be back in a minute. I'm only goin' down as far as the shop.

CONWAY. Well listen, leave us the key of the closet before you go will yeh. We'll have a quick game of snooker first.

PADDY. The closet is open. Stapler is in there already sure.

CONWAY (*turns to* TONY). Where's the other fella tonight?

TONY. He's out in the jacks.

CONWAY. I see him down in the factory today and he all done up like a dog's dinner. He must have had an interview on or somethin', did he Tony?

TONY. I don't know.

CONWAY. Oh yeah, you're an auld gom too.

TONY. I don't know, Conway.

CONWAY. I'm not coddin' yeh Paddy, he has a neck on him now like a jockey's bollocks, the same fella.

PADDY (*buttoning up his overcoat*). Who's that?

CONWAY. Jimmy Brady. I say he was down in the factory for an interview or somethin' today and he spent the best part of his time now chattin' up the young one in the office.

PADDY *gives a little dismissive nod.*

A great suit and tie and all on him Paddy. I'm not coddin' yeh, to look at him you'd swear butter wouldn't melt in his mouth.

STAPLER (*peeping out of the back room*). Hey Paddy get us a bar of Aero and yeh down there will yeh.

PADDY. Yeah right.

CONWAY. Well Stapler what do you think of the boy here?

STAPLER. What about him?

CONWAY. Do yeh hear Stapler, what about him? He's for the high jump that's what about him.

STAPLER. What do yeh mean?

CONWAY (*sings and mimes playing a violin*).

The bells are ringing for me and my girl
The parson's waiting for me and my girl . . .

STAPLER'*s face saddens at this news.*

Young Whelan.

STAPLER. Who?

CONWAY. Bandy's daughter. Yeh know Bandy. Here's me head and me arse is comin'. (*He demonstrates a duck-like walk.*) The only man I know who is capable of being in two places at the one time.

STAPLER. So are yeh gettin' married then Tony?

TONY (*sighs*). I don't know. I suppose so.

CONWAY. What do you mean, yeh suppose so? You renege on that little girl, boy, and Bandy Whelan will have your guts for garters, so he will. Hey Stapler some of the lads were sayin' that he was cryin' in the canteen this mornin'.

STAPLER. Sure that's no harm.

CONWAY. Well I've no sympathy for him Stapler. He dipped his wick and now he must pay for the pleasure. What did I say to you this time last year Tony?

TONY. You said if my gate creaked I was to make sure and oil it myself before somebody else did it for me.

CONWAY. Yeah and what else did I say?

TONY. Get them young and they'll fly with yeh.

CONWAY. Be careful, I said, or you'll end up buyin' a pram on the never never.

TONY. Oh yeah I forgot about that.

CONWAY. I know you did. Otherwise you wouldn't be in this predicament would yeh?

JIMMY *swaggers out of the toilet. He strikes a match off the edge of the pool table and lights up a scut of a fag that is wedged behind his ear. He sits up on the pool table, his legs dangling.*

Here he is now. Cool Hand Luke.

PADDY (*on his way out of the front door*). If he don't stop strikin' matches off of my good table I'll Cool Hand Luke him.

CONWAY (*moving closer to* JIMMY). Well boy did yeh get the job after?

JIMMY. What job?

CONWAY. I heard you were lookin' for a job down below.

JIMMY. I wouldn't work in a kip like that if you paid me.

CONWAY. Yeah, well I wouldn't worry about that if I was you 'cause I'd safely say there's very little chance of them takin' you on . . . It was short and sweet anyway wasn't it?

JIMMY. What was?

CONWAY. The interview.

JIMMY. Yeah. I took one good look out the window and I saw all these grown men walkin' around dressed up like peasants and I decided there and then that it wasn't the like for me after all.

CONWAY *opens up his overcoat to reveal his overalls.*

CONWAY. It takes a good man to fill one of these boy and don't you ever forget it.

JIMMY *reaches across and tugs roughly at* CONWAY's *overall around the groin area.*

JIMMY. I'd say it's a queer long time since you went next or near to fillin' that up then is it?

CONWAY. Hey, don't let the grey hairs fool yeh poor man.

JIMMY. It's not just the grey hairs Conway. It's the bags under the eyes and the green teeth and the fat belly . . .

CONWAY (*trying to conceal his annoyance*). I'll tell yeh one thing, no woman in this town ever gave me the bum's rush anyway. Hey Stapler, 'I'm washin' me hair', says she to him.

STAPLER. Who?

CONWAY. Linda in the office down below. Your man here asked her for a date. 'I'm washin' me hair', says she. I'm washin' me hair. The oldest one in the book. Honest to God.

JIMMY. Of course she's washin' her hair. I'd told her she'd have to clean herself up before I had anythin' to do with her.

CONWAY. Yes, yeh did yeah. You wouldn't even be in the runnin' there boy. That one wouldn't even contemplate dancin' with the likes of you. You'd have to have a biro stickin' up out of your top pocket before that one would even admit that you existed at all. So don't go foolin' yourself into believin' otherwise.

JIMMY. Will you go and cop on to yourself Conway. There's nothin' special about her.

CONWAY. Do yeh hear . . . Lawrence of Arabia where he is.

STAPLER. Come on Conway and I'll give yeh a game of snooker.

CONWAY. Yeah right Stapler, I'll be in there in a minute.

STAPLER *goes into the back room.* CONWAY *heads for the toilet.*

JIMMY. Oh that reminds me Conway, I'm wantin' fifty pence off you.

CONWAY. You'll be lucky.

JIMMY. We're runnin' a bus down to see Stapler kickin' the shit out of your man tomorrow night.

CONWAY *throws him a dirty look over his shoulder before he goes out.*

TONY. Conway thinks that your man Harpur will beat Stapler.

JIMMY *thinks about it.*

JIMMY. What the fuck would he know about it.

JIMMY *circles the table sizing up his next shot. He sprawls himself across the table just as* PADDY *enters with a handful of things. He is not too pleased to see* JIMMY *stretched across the table.*

PADDY (*shuffling towards the back room*). You get down off that table boy.

JIMMY. Stop the noise Paddy, this is a complicated shot.

PADDY. Yeah well, use the rest.

JIMMY *ignores him and takes his shot.* PADDY *watches and silently scoffs at the boy's lack of skill.* PADDY *goes into the back room just as* CONWAY *is coming out of the toilet.*

JIMMY. Hey Conway are yeh wantin' to take on the winner?

CONWAY. Look I told you before boy. You put up a nice crisp five pound note and I'll take you on, no bother. Moolay, that's my language. I mean to say there's no point in me givin' out lessons to every Tom, Dick and Harry who comes along if there's nothin' in it for me now is there?

JIMMY. I'll tell yeh what I'll do with yeh now Conway. I'll bet you a pound that Stapler beats your man tomorrow night.

CONWAY (*diving into his pocket, pulling out a pound*). You're on. Put your money down there.

JIMMY. Well, I haven't got it on me at the moment but . . .

CONWAY. Hey . . . no mon, no fun boy. If you want to bet with me put your money down on the table there. Otherwise forget it. None of this 'I'll see you Monday' lark at all.

TONY. I'd say Stapler will be well able for your man.

CONWAY. Well there's a pound note says he won't.

TONY. I'll tell yeh one thing Conway he's trainin' queer hard for it.

CONWAY. Yes he is yeah. The only thing Stapler is fit for now is the high jump.

TONY. What do you mean?

CONWAY (*glancing over his shoulder to make sure that* STAPLER *is not there in the doorway or anywhere in sight*). Look he's down in The Shark every night now – drinkin' and knockin' around with your one.

TONY. What one?

CONWAY. The big one do be down there. The one that plays the jukebox all the time.

TONY *looks puzzled*.

She's a hairdresser. A nice bit of stuff.

TONY. I don't know her at all. And Stapler is knockin' her off is he?

CONWAY. Stapler is knockin' around with her this ages.

TONY. And do she know he's married?

CONWAY. Of course she knows he's married. Sure she wouldn't mind that.

TONY. I can't place her at all. Do you know her Jimmy?

JIMMY. Yeah. She's a big fat one. She's rotten.

CONWAY (*sweeping up his money*). So as soon as any of you boys wants to put your money where your mouth is, just give me a shout. (*He heads towards the back room.*)

TONY. Give us a fag Conway before yeh go will yeh?

CONWAY (*stopping in the doorway*). Do you ever buy fags at all boy? I'm not coddin' yeah, he's the very same in work. I'm like a mother to him that's all. Oh here, with your Vincent de Paul face on yeh.

CONWAY *tosses* TONY *a cigarette. Enter* LINDA, *peeping around the door.*

JIMMY (*spotting her*). Here she is now. Now say what you were sayin' about her.

CONWAY (*a little flustered*). What?

LINDA (*stepping forward with contempt*). Why, who was talkin' about me Jimmy?

CONWAY. Yeah Tony, now say what you were sayin' about the girl.

TONY. What?

LINDA (*moving towards him*). Hey Tony, what were you sayin' about me?

TONY. Don't mind them, I never said nothin' . . .

CONWAY. You should be ashamed of yourself, talkin' about the little girl like that behind her back.

JIMMY. Tony is gone all red.

LINDA *seems to cop what has been going on and throws a dagger of a look in* CONWAY's *direction.* PADDY *is gazing out at her through the glass panel, a vexed expression on his face.* LINDA *glares back at him.* JIMMY *follows her gaze, traces it back to* PADDY.

Hey Linda I told yeh not to be followin' me around didn't I. I mean I come in here to get away from women. And look at the state of poor Paddy with yeh. He's nearly after havin' a hernia in there. I mean to say Paddy don't even like lads with long hair comin' in here, never mind girls.

LINDA. It's a pity about him.

JIMMY. Anyway Linda I told you today that I wasn't goin' out with yeh, so don't keep askin' me.

LINDA *gives a little husky laugh.* JIMMY *bends to shoot, coming up to find her looking into his eyes. He softens.*

What's wrong with yeh hon?

LINDA. I just popped in to tell yeh that I'll be late comin' down tonight. I'm only goin' up home now. I had to do a bit of overtime.

JIMMY. Yeh mean to tell me you haven't cleaned yourself up yet?

LINDA *sighs.*

Do yeh want me to come up to the house for yeh?

LINDA. Yeah, if you like.

JIMMY. Yeah, I don't mind.

She smiles at his tenderness, goes across to check out the jukebox.

CONWAY. Were you workin' overtime tonight Linda?

LINDA. What? Yeah.

CONWAY. What are yeh goin' to do with it all eh?

LINDA. All what?

CONWAY. All this money you're makin'?

LINDA. I'm goin' to tell yeh one thing Conway, if I had half as much in the bank as you have I wouldn't be workin' at all. I'd retire to the Bahamas or somewhere.

CONWAY. Half as much as me? You must be jokin'.

LINDA. Go away out of that Conway, you're coinin' out of that factory so yeh are. Sure you're workin' practically every night of the week.

CONWAY. They can't do without me Linda. I'm a good worker yeh know?

JIMMY. A good lick-arse would be more like it.

LINDA. Aw lads these are all ancient . . . The Hucklebuck.

TONY. Hey Linda, what happened about the generator after?

JIMMY. What generator?

TONY. Somebody knocked off the generator down there. Sure did yeh not notice the cops swarmin' all over the place today?

JIMMY. I saw Swan snoopin' around alright. I'd say he was dyin' to know what was I doin' down there.

LINDA. He asked me about yeh. He said he saw yeh comin' out of the office.

JIMMY. What did you say to him?

LINDA. I told him you had an interview.

JIMMY. The nosy bastard.

TONY. I heard they found the generator in the boot of O'Brien's car. Did you hear anythin' about that Conway?

CONWAY (*emphatically*). No.

JIMMY. Who's O'Brien, the Manager?

TONY. No, the Works Foreman – the fella that interviewed you.

JIMMY. I thought he was the Manager.

TONY. No, he's only the Works Foreman.

JIMMY. And they found it in his boot did they?

TONY. So I heard.

JIMMY. What was he doin', knockin' it off?

TONY. I don't know.

JIMMY. And he was lookin' down his nose at me.

TONY. Some of the lads were sayin' that he'll probably get the shove now.

JIMMY (*thinks about it*). Naw, that'll be all hushed up.

CONWAY. What would you say Linda?

LINDA. I'd say he was probably takin' it home to clean it.

CONWAY *laughs at her sarcastic tone of voice*. TONY *follows suit*.

CONWAY. Hey Linda, it's a wonder yeh wouldn't put a word in for the boy here down below.

LINDA. What?

CONWAY. I say, it's a wonder yeh wouldn't try to get Jimmy that job that's goin' down in the factory. Sure you're well in with your man O'Brien, ain't yeh?

LINDA. Yes, I am yeah.

CONWAY. Aw now yeh are Linda. Every time I go in there you're sittin' on his lap.

TONY. Hey Linda, what's this all about?

LINDA. I wouldn't mind sittin' on the man's lap at all Tony. The only thing is Conway is always there before me. I'm not coddin' yeh lads, everytime I turn around he's standin' there. He's hauntin' the office that's all.

JIMMY. Sure, that's nothin' Linda. When I was in there havin' the interview Conway's tongue came slidin' in under the door. Quick as yeh can say O'Brien to me, get your back to the wall . . .

The others laugh.

CONWAY. There was only one thing O'Brien ever said to you Jimmy. GET LOST.

JIMMY. Yeh can't get lost when yeh know your way around, Conway. (*He sings.*)

Dawdling through this shoddy, shabby town
You can't get lost when you know your way around.

TONY *joins in, using the cue as a guitar.*

I'm the king of the renegades
I'm as sharp as a razor blade
Worry if you want
But don't you worry about me . . .

PADDY *is looking out at them, frowning.*

JIMMY. What do yeh think of that Linda? Tony is queer good on that cue ain't he?

LINDA (*smiles*). I'll see yeh later on Jimmy.

JIMMY. Yeah right. I'll be up in about an hour or so.

LINDA (*over her shoulder*). Tell the auld lad I said goodbye to him. (*She leaves, closing the door behind her.*)

JIMMY (*shouts after her*). Don't forget to wash your hair. (*He goes smirking around the table.*) Yeh see Conway, some of us just have it. Yeh know what I mean?

CONWAY. Yeah, and I think we can all safely say that you're certainly full of it.

JIMMY *laughs.* CONWAY *goes into the back room smiling a sick smile.*

JIMMY. What do yeh think of her Tony?

TONY. She's nice, boy.

JIMMY. Conway's ragin'. He's some headache ain't he?

TONY. Aw, he's alright.

JIMMY. He gets on my nerves.

TONY. Would yeh say he's tellin' the truth about Stapler, knockin' around with your one I mean?

JIMMY. I don't know. I suppose so. Fellas like Conway are never too far off the mark. Not when it comes to somebody else's downfall anyway.

TONY. How do yeh mean?

JIMMY. Sure Stapler's a martyr for the women. I heard big Jack Larkin came home one day and discovered Stapler's shoes under his bed. There was war I heard.

TONY. How did he know they were Stapler's?

JIMMY. A scruffy pair of Beatle boots. Who else wears them in this town any more, only Stapler.

TONY. Yeah, well that's no proof that Stapler was actually in the bed with big Jack's missus though, is it?

JIMMY. I don't know. It'd do me anyway.

TONY. Yeah, but it's not definite proof, is it?

JIMMY. What are you wantin' Tony, a fuckin' video or somethin'?

TONY. No. All I'm sayin' is that you can't be a hundred per cent sure, that's all.

JIMMY *shakes his head in disbelief.*

There's no use jumpin' the gun Jimmy . . . I think Mrs Larkin is a terribly nice woman.

JIMMY *sighs.*

JIMMY (*drawing closer*). Look Tony, let me put it this way, if I ever get the chance of takin' off me shoes in big Joan Larkin's bedroom when Jack is out workin' somewhere I'd say there's a fair chance that me pants will fall down not too shortly after.

TONY. Yeah, well if yeh put it like that . . .

JIMMY. Yeah!

TONY. Yeh'd never hear Stapler talkin' about women though.

JIMMY. He's probably savin' his energy.

TONY *can't believe it. He lights up a cigarette, takes a couple of quick drags and hands it across to* JIMMY. TONY *takes his shot and reclaims his cigarette again. As* JIMMY *rambles around the table* TONY *inches his way closer to the glass panel. He watches with envy and fascination the activity inside, a big broad grin appearing on his face. When it is his turn to shoot he is in a trance and* JIMMY *becomes annoyed with him.*

(*Angrily.*) Are you playin' or not Tony?

TONY (*startled*). What? Oh Yeah, right! Did yeh ever see the chair Conway sits in Jimmy?

JIMMY. What about it?

TONY. It's got a big cushion and all, and a great big back to it. It looks like a throne, don't it? Do yeh know what, boy it must be great to play on that big snooker table inside there. It looks deadly and even or somethin' . . . Stapler says that it takes a queer long time to get used to it too. He says . . .

JIMMY (*narky*). Yeah, well never mind all that. We're out here not in there. So take your shot and stop dreamin' will yeh.

TONY *reverts back to the bad cue, seeing that* JIMMY *hasn't offered him the good one.* TONY *chalks up.*

What are yeh always lookin' in there for anyway?

TONY. Why? There's no law against lookin' is there?

JIMMY (*sneeringly*). No, but lookin' won't get yeh in there, will it Tony?

TONY *is a little embarrassed now. He takes his shot, coming up to find* JIMMY *standing in front of the glass panel, blatantly watching with obvious scorn the goings on inside.*

TONY. I don't know what you're goin' on about anyway Jimmy, you're lookin' in there now.

JIMMY (*turning slowly to face his friend*). Yeah I know I am but not the way you were.

TONY. What do yeh mean?

JIMMY. You know well enough what I mean. My shot is it?

TONY (*feeling belittled*). Yeah.

JIMMY *sighs, takes a long look at* TONY *and approaches the table shaking his head and smirking.*

(*Offended.*) What's wrong with you Jimmy?

JIMMY (*smirks*). Nothin'.

TONY. I think you're crackin' up boy.

As JIMMY *moves around the table, sizing up what is left,* TONY *steals another glimpse into the back room, finding it irresistible.*

Lights down.

Scene Two

The Club with the back room full and a big game on. PADDY *is sweeping the outside area.* JIMMY *staggers in drunk. He has a naggon of whiskey under his coat. He takes a slug, coughs and splutters.* PADDY *throws him a dirty look.*

JIMMY (*oblivious to* PADDY's *scorn*). Hey Paddy, did you see Tony anywhere?

PADDY. No.

JIMMY. He wasn't in here, no?

PADDY. No.

JIMMY. I wonder where he is? He must be on the job somewhere Paddy?

PADDY. Hey boy what's that you're drinkin'?

JIMMY. It's Lourdes' water Paddy. Do you want a drop? Hey Paddy what's all this about?

PADDY. What?

JIMMY has spied that the top of PADDY's *underpants is sticking out and he has his shirt and gansy tucked down inside it.* JIMMY *goes over and tugs at it annoyingly.*

JIMMY. This. That's indecent that is, I hope you know. You should be ashamed of yourself Paddy. Paradin' around like that and showin' your drawers off. Supposin' a couple of young ones walked in here now. You'd drive them into a frenzy, so you would.

PADDY *breaks loose. He is not amused.*

PADDY. That'll do yeh now boy.

JIMMY (*laughs*). Ah, don't mind me Paddy. Sure you're worse yourself. Here have a drink.

PADDY (*curtly*). No thanks.

JIMMY. Go on, have a slug.

PADDY. I told yeh, I don't want one.

JIMMY. Alright Paddy keep your shirt on.

JIMMY takes another slug of whiskey, lays the bottle on the edge of the pool table, picks up a cue and begins tapping around a few balls.

What ails yeh anyway Paddy? Are you sick or somethin'? I heard you'd drink it off a sore leg.

PADDY *moves towards* JIMMY, *pulling the cue away from him.*

PADDY. Give me that here before you tear the cloth on me. Go on out of here, the hell out of that.

PADDY *puts the cue back in the cue stand.* JIMMY *sits up on the table defiantly.*

JIMMY (*slurring his words*). No listen though Paddy, was Tony in here tonight? Straight up now Paddy, this is important. I swear.

PADDY. Off with yeh now.

JIMMY. What? Oh yeah, right Paddy. I'm goin' in a minute. But listen if Tony comes in here tell him I'm lookin' all over the place for him will yeh? Tell him I'll be down in the Shark. No, tell him I'll meet him in . . . (*He turns his head to discover that* PADDY *is not listening to him at all and has ambled into the back room.* JIMMY *calls after him.*)

Hey Paddy, that reminds me. Is Conway in there? Tell him I'm wantin' to talk to him will yeh?

JIMMY *rummages through his pockets, pulling out a wad of pound notes. A handful of small change falls onto the floor and* JIMMY *doesn't even bother to pick it up. He staggers towards the back room and pushes the door ajar.*

Hey Conway. Come on out here.

PADDY (*coming to the door, blocking* JIMMY's *view*). What are you at there?

JIMMY. Tell Conway I'm wantin' him will yeh?

PADDY. He's in a game.

JIMMY. What? Yeah, well just tell him I'm wantin' to see him for a minute.

PADDY. I told yeh, he's in a game.

JIMMY. Never mind the game. Tell him Jimmy Brady is out here. Tell him I've a tenner, says that I . . . (no tell him a tenner though . . . a tenner says that). I can beat him. On this table or the one inside, whichever he likes. It makes no difference to me tell him. Here come out of me way. I'll tell him myself. (*He tries to slip in but* PADDY *blocks the way with his arms.*) Just a second Paddy. I just want a quick word with him that's all. I swear it won't take a second. A minute at the most.

PADDY (*holding* JIMMY *at arms' length*). No way boy.

JIMMY (*fuming*). You're some fuckin' louser Paddy. You see the way Conway's always shootin' off his big maw mouth when meself and Tony are tryin' to have a game here. And now you won't even . . . Here Conway, come out here yeh spastic yeh till I whitewash yeh . . . (*He is pushing against* PADDY *now, trying to break* PADDY's *grip on the doorframe.*)

PADDY. Hey boy hey. Can you not read or what?

JIMMY. What? Yeah, of course I can read. Why?

PADDY (*pointing to the sign stabbing it with his finger*). Members only.

JIMMY. Yeah Okay. Paddy, I'll join. How much do you want? What do I have to do to . . .

PADDY. Look the best thing you can do now is get out of here before you destroy the feckin' place on me. Go on the hell out of that. (*He is really angry now and pushes* JIMMY *away from the door viciously.*)

JIMMY. Alright Paddy, take it easy. Cut out the shovin'. What have you got in there anyway that's so precious? You'd think it was Fort Knox or somethin' the way you go on.

PADDY. Go ahead home now or wherever the hell it is you're goin'.

JIMMY. Yeah alright Paddy, I'm goin' in a minute and then you can stick this place up your arse.

PADDY. That'll do yeh now boy.

JIMMY *defies* PADDY *and sits up on the pool table, taking another slug of whiskey, belching loudly.*

You go on about your business now me man.

JIMMY. Alright Paddy, stop fussin' will yeh before you give your heart a hernia.

PADDY. Well go then.

JIMMY. Yeah, I'm goin' in a minute I said.

PADDY *sighs, goes into the back room again, shutting the door tight behind him.* JIMMY's *head turns at the sound of the door closing. He takes a long, hard look at the place before turning his back to it, taking another gulp of whiskey. We catch a glimpse of* CONWAY *looking out through the glass panel at him.* JIMMY *begins to hiccup. Enter* STAPLER *with a bandage on his nose.*

JIMMY. Oon Stapler me boy.

STAPLER. How's it goin' son?

JIMMY. Flyin' Stapler. I'm flyin' so I am.

STAPLER. Yeah, you look like a fella that's flyin' alright. What are yeh doin', celebratin' or somethin'?

JIMMY. What? Yeah I'm celebratin'. It's Paddy's birthday. He's a hundred and four today. Hey Stapler, look at the state of him in there. He looks like an auld scarecrow, don't he? Yeh know what, it'd be great to dress Paddy up wouldn't it? I'd love to see him in a real skin tight jeans, would you? And his hair slicked back like Elvis. Oh yeah, and one of those little three quarter length rock and roll coats on him – yeh know the ones with the furry collars. And he playin' the jukebox down in the Shark . . . (*The story is almost incomprehensible because* JIMMY, *who seems to find it hilariously funny, is laughing so much.*) And one of those little skinny ties on him ha ha . . .

STAPLER. What is that you're drinkin'? Jungle juice or somethin'?

JIMMY. What? Here, have a slug.

STAPLER. No thanks. I'm bad enough. So how did you get on with Linda after boy? Did you take her out or what?

JIMMY. No, she took me out.

STAPLER. She took you.

JIMMY. Yeah. Sure I hadn't got a button Stapler.

STAPLER. So she paid did she?

JIMMY. Yeah, she brought me to the pictures. I'm supposed to be meetin' her tonight too. What time is it anyway Stapler?

STAPLER. It's about twenty past nine I'd say.

JIMMY *makes a face.*

Why, what time are you supposed to meet her?

JIMMY. Half seven. (*He laughs and hides behind his own hand.*)

STAPLER. You'll be shot.

JIMMY *thinks about it and shrugs it off.*

JIMMY. Hey Stapler I'll tell yeh one thing boy, your hair looks queer well this weather.

STAPLER. What?

JIMMY. Your hair.

STAPLER. What about it?

JIMMY. I say it looks queer snazzy. Of course I heard you're gettin' it done for nothin' – now is that right? I'm warnin' yeh Stapler, I've me eye on you. I'm watching' yeh boy.

STAPLER *moves towards the back room.*

Oh, that reminds me. I owe you a pound don't I?

JIMMY *pulls out the wad of notes and peels off a pound and hands it across to* STAPLER. STAPLER *is flabbergasted at the amount of money* JIMMY *has.*

STAPLER. What's all this?

JIMMY. I won this last night on a boxin' match. I backed a fella called Eddie Harpur. He was fightin' this auld fucker last night yeh know? He nearly killed him too. Broke his nose and everything.

STAPLER *is tongue-tied with anger now. He pockets the pound note and makes to leave.*

I'm goin' to tell you one thing Stapler, it's a good job I didn't put me few bob on you last night, that's all. I'd have been up after you this mornin' to bate the back off yeh with a big hurl or somethin'.

STAPLER *heads towards the back room, crestfallen.*

Hey Stapler.

STAPLER (*in the doorway*). What?

JIMMY. You should have ducked.

STAPLER *is not amused. He goes to say something but changes his mind.* JIMMY *is stuffing the money back into his pocket, seemingly unaware of* STAPLER's *discomfort and annoyance.* STAPLER *eventually leaves him there, disappearing into the back room.* JIMMY *finds himself alone again. He sits up on the pool table, hangs his head and sighs, slipping into a kind of a trance.* CONWAY *comes out of the*

back room and goes into the toilet, stopping on his way to have a look at
JIMMY who doesn't realise that CONWAY is there. When CONWAY
is gone JIMMY gets up and goes across to the glass panel. He watches
the men inside mumbling and arguing as the smoke wafts and curls all
around them. Then JIMMY turns his back on the scene as he takes a
look around at the outside area, swigging another slug of whiskey. He
pulls a sickly face, plonks the bottle down on the shelf and staggers out
the door. PADDY hears the door bang and comes out to check what's
going on. CONWAY comes out of the toilet.

CONWAY. Paddy, give us a toilet roll there will yeh?

PADDY. What? Why is there none in there?

CONWAY. No.

PADDY. Right. Hang on there and I'll ah . . .

PADDY goes into the back room leaving CONWAY yawning and
scratching. CONWAY spots some money on the floor and bends down to
pick it up. He pockets it smiling to himself. PADDY comes back with the
toilet roll.

CONWAY. Is the other fella gone Paddy or what?

PADDY. Yeah, he's gone. A bloody nuisance that lad is.

CONWAY. Oh, you'd be better off without him altogether Paddy.

PADDY. What? Yeah.

CONWAY. Because sooner or later he's goin' to cause more
trouble than he's worth. Yeh know what I mean Paddy?

CONWAY takes the toilet roll and goes back into the toilet. PADDY
spies some money up by the pool table. He picks it up, counts it and
pockets it, showing no expression of pleasure.

Enter SWAN just as PADDY is going into the back room. SWAN
stands in the doorway and takes a long, hard look at the place,
wondering what on earth anyone in his right mind could see in it.
PADDY peers out through the glass panel and shuffles out to see what
he wants.

SWAN (*circling the table, scrutinising the place*). Well Paddy. How are
you?

PADDY. Not too bad.

SWAN. Good. So how's business with yeh Paddy?

PADDY. Alright.

SWAN. What's that?

PADDY. Okay.

SWAN. Keepin' the wolf away from the door, as they say Paddy.

PADDY. Yeah.

SWAN. Good begor. Is this a new cloth you got on the table or what?

PADDY. Yeah.

SWAN (*feeling the smoothness of the cloth on the pool table*). I thought that. Expensive enough articles too I'd say.

PADDY. Yeah. They're dear alright.

SWAN. Well, anything strange or startling to tell me at all?

PADDY (*thinks about it*). No.

SWAN (*irritably*). What's that?

PADDY. No, I haven't.

SWAN *goes over to the blackboard and takes a look at the names that are scrawled there, squinting up at the writing.*

SWAN. G. Sanders. Who would that be now Paddy? G. Sanders.

PADDY *becomes flustered, moves closer to the blackboard, taking out his glasses and putting them on.*

PADDY. Who?

SWAN. This lad here look. G. Sanders. What Sanders would he be?

PADDY. Aw, young Sanders yeah. He gets in here alright. Now and again like, yeh know.

SWAN. Yes. (*Pause.*) Who is he? Ernie's young lad, is it?

PADDY. No. Tony Sanders would be his Da . . . Ah I wouldn't say you'd know him.

SWAN. Tony above in King Street there. Yes I do know him. I know him well sure. He works on the railway?

PADDY. Yeah.

SWAN. I know Tony alright. I didn't think he had a lad old enough to come in here though. (*He stares at the old man and there is a long embarrassing silence. PADDY turns his eyes away from*

SWAN, *gazing at the floor one minute, towards the back room the next, not knowing where to look*.) Well Paddy, tell me this and tell me no more, what I wanted to ask you. Was there by any chance a young fella in here tonight with plenty of money. Money to burn in fact?

PADDY. No, I didn't notice anyone.

SWAN. He'd have a fair few jars in him too, I'd say. Drunk more than likely.

PADDY. No.

SWAN. Quiet all night was it?

PADDY. Yeah, it was fairly quiet alright.

SWAN. Nobody staggered in here loaded and flashing it about, no?

PADDY. No, I didn't see . . .

SWAN *drums his fingers on the edge of the table.*

SWAN. You didn't notice anything unusual, no?

PADDY. No.

SWAN. Tell me Paddy, what time did you open up tonight?

PADDY. It was fairly late. I went up as far as the pictures. I'd say it must have been twenty to nine or thereabouts.

SWAN (*considers the answer*). Twenty to nine. Yeah. (*Pause.*) Do you like the pictures Paddy?

PADDY. I do, yeah.

SWAN. They're dyin' out too I think.

PADDY. They are. The auld television is killin' them sure.

SWAN. Yes. It is indeed.

STAPLER (*appearing in the doorway of the back room*). Paddy, give us another deck of cards there will yeh when you're ready.

PADDY. What? Oh yeah, right. I'll be in there now in a minute.

SWAN. Poor Stapler. How is he since his ordeal?

PADDY. Aw he's alright.

SWAN. He got a right smack too I believe. Fractured is it?

PADDY. No, it's broken.

SWAN (*wincing in sympathy*). That'll be sore then.

CONWAY *comes out of the toilet, surprised to see* SWAN *there.*

Well boy are yeh makin' any money at all this weather?

CONWAY. Naw. Holdin' me own as the fella said.

SWAN. You must be slippin' up.

CONWAY. Aw sure you know yourself.

SWAN. What was I goin' to say to yeh . . .

CONWAY *reluctantly comes nearer.*

Em . . . oh yeah . . . did I see you the other day down
below?

CONWAY. Where? Oh in the factory. Sure I'm workin' down
there.

SWAN. Oh I know you work in the factory but I thought I caught
a glimpse of you in the maintenance room. Have you been
shifted or somethin'?

CONWAY. What? Aw no. Sure that's Stapler's department. No I
was just in there to see the lads about something that's all.

SWAN. I was wonderin'. I was just sayin' to Paddy here, poor
Stapler got a right smack.

CONWAY. Yeah. But sure that young Harpur chap is brilliant.
He's on the way up now too. He'll pull an Irish title this year I'd
say. If he don't do it this year he'll definitely get it next year. No
doubt about it.

PADDY *takes advantage of this conversation and creeps off into the
back room closing the door over after him.* SWAN's *eyes follow* PADDY
into the back room.

Stapler is gone too hardy for that lark now.

SWAN. What?

CONWAY. I say Stapler is too . . . You'd want to be a young lad
for that game.

SWAN. You would. Paddy's a queer hawk, ain't he?

CONWAY. Who? Paddy? Yeah, he's a queer fella alright.

SWAN. I can't make him out at all.

CONWAY. How's that?

SWAN. Well I mean, he knows well enough that I'm lookin' for a young lad who caused a bit of trouble up town earlier on – well he caused a lot of trouble actually, but however – and I know for a fact that he has been in here already tonight. But Paddy wouldn't budge on it at all. He lied to me. I don't like that kind of thing. I know chaps will be chaps and all the rest of it but I'm lookin' for this fella. Sooner or later a boy has to learn to toe the line. Paddy can't see that. Can you see that?

CONWAY. What? Oh yeah, I can see that . . .

SWAN. Do you agree with me?

CONWAY. Oh I agree with yeh. I mean sooner or later a young lad has to . . .

SWAN. I mean I've more things to be doin' now than pullin' and prisin' young lads off of jukeboxes and young ones or whatever the hell else they get up to. (*Pause.*) I'll find him anyway. All I have to do is to narrow it down to the lads who were in here tonight, pick two or three likely candidates and bingo . . .

CONWAY (*takes a stealthy look around*). There wasn't very many in here tonight. It was terrible quiet. I mean . . . (*He sighs, takes a glance over his shoulder, forgives himself and carries on.*) . . . the only one I saw in here tonight was Jimmy Brady. He was in here about half eight or thereabouts.

SWAN (*smiling to himself*). Jimmy Brady. I thought it was near time he came out of hidin' alright.

CONWAY. I'm not sayin' it was him now that did it. He was in here tonight, that's all I'm sayin'.

SWAN. Was he drunk?

CONWAY. He had a good few jars in him alright.

SWAN. Did you see his hands?

CONWAY. I never said that it was him that did it now. All I said was . . .

SWAN. Never mind. It was him alright. It has Jimmy Brady stamped all over it. Well there'll be a nice little holiday in this for him then.

He makes to leave, making a detour to say farewell to PADDY.
PADDY *sees him coming and comes out to cut him off.*

I'll go Paddy.

PADDY. Are yeh off?

SWAN. Yeah. (*He finds the bottle that* JIMMY BRADY *has left behind him. He picks it up, smells it, rolls it around, spots the red stains on it, lays it back down on the shelf gingerly to avoid the ink.*) Somebody hittin' the bottle Paddy. I'll see yeh lads.

PADDY. All the best.

CONWAY. Good luck.

SWAN *walks towards the front door, stopping in the open doorway.*

SWAN. Oh by the way Paddy, did yeh know someone is after gettin' sick all over your top step here?

PADDY. What? Where?

SWAN. Outside there. You'd want to clean it before somebody slips on it and gives himself a right toss.

SWAN *leaves. Pause.* PADDY *gets some old newspaper from in under the bench.*

CONWAY. That's a nosy whore that fella is, Paddy.

Lights down.

Scene Three

The Club a few nights later in darkness. There is some commotion off stage and soon JIMMY *comes into view, coming out of the toilet door. He goes across to the front door and opens it up.* LINDA *steps in,* JIMMY *closing the door gently behind her and switching on the light.* LINDA *stands just inside the door, looking around at the place, seemingly unimpressed.* JIMMY *goes across to the pot-bellied stove and starts banking it up with coal.*

LINDA. I thought you said you had your own key.

JIMMY. No I said meself and Tony had our own private entrance.

LINDA (*moving a little deeper into the club*). Oh! . . . How did you get in as a matter of interest?

JIMMY. What? There's a window broken in the jacks. It's been like that this ages. Meself and Tony let ourselves in and out of here whenever we've no place else to go. It's queer handy.

LINDA. Won't someone see the light shinin' from the street?

JIMMY. No. We checked that out. I had Tony stand down there one night and look up. Once those shutters arc drawn you can't tell a thing.

LINDA. You have it well planned. All the same I think I'd prefer to be somewhere else.

JIMMY. Look stop fussin'. I told yeh it was alright. (JIMMY *rubs his hands together and stands up.*) A bit of heat now and we'll be elected. Poor Paddy will be hoverin' over this yoke tomorrow night, tryin' to figure out where all the coal is gone. I'm not coddin' yeh, meself and Tony were often here breakin' our hearts laughin' and Paddy looking at the half empty bucket and scratchin' himself. We'd be after usin' all the coal up on him.

LINDA. Oh now you're a right pair of chancers.

JIMMY *sits on the bench. He watches her ramble around the club, touching the cues, caressing the table and finally coming to a standstill in front of the glass panel. She tries to see in but it is too dark.*

JIMMY. What do yeh think of it?

LINDA. What's in there? The auld fella's office or somethin'?

JIMMY. What? No that's where the whatdoyoucallit go . . . the élite.

LINDA. The élite?

JIMMY. Yeah. Conway and all.

She cups her hands and peers in. JIMMY *rambles over closer to her, standing behind her.*

That's Tony's main ambition yeh know?

LINDA. What is?

JIMMY. To get inside there.

LINDA (*ponders on the remark*). Why don't he just break in there some night when the pair of yeh have the run of the place?

JIMMY. That's what I said. But no, that wouldn't do him at all.

LINDA. Why not?

JIMMY (*thinks about it*). Tony's waitin' to be invited in.

LINDA. Invited? Who's goin' to invite him?

JIMMY (*putting on a deep voice*). The men. (*He steps up to the slot machine and puts some money in, banging away at it.*) It's not just gettin' in there that matters to him yeh know? It's ah . . . I don't know.

LINDA. He wants to be accepted I suppose?

JIMMY. Yeah.

LINDA (*sarcastically*). By the men?

JIMMY. I suppose so.

LINDA *smirks at the very idea.*

LINDA (*taking down a cue, awkwardly taps around with a few loose balls that have been left on the table*). And what about you?

JIMMY. Me? What about me?

LINDA. You mean to tell me you don't dream about gettin' in there too?

JIMMY (*smiles at this remark*). Naw . . . I don't belong in there.

LINDA. Where do you belong then?

JIMMY. What? Where? I don't know. Not in there anyway that's for sure.

JIMMY *is standing close to her now and the intimacy seems to make LINDA uneasy. She breaks away, placing the cue across the table.*

LINDA. What's in there?

JIMMY. The jacks.

LINDA *backs out of the doorway, cringing at the stink of the place. She spots a cutting from a newspaper pinned up on the door that leads to the back room. She goes across to read it. JIMMY picks up the cue and starts to show off, taking up an exaggerated stance sprawling himself across the table.*

LINDA. 'Chase over rooftops.' (*She glances towards him.*)

JIMMY (*takes his shot*). 'A dramatic chase took place last Sunday night over rooftops on the South Main Street when a young man

who was suspected of breaking and entering was pursued by
Detective Garda Swan. The drama occurred when Detective
Swan slipped and went tumbling down the slanted roof. Eye
witnesses said that he was dangling from a considerable height,
holding on to the gutter by the tips of his fingers. Ah . . .'

LINDA. 'His cries for help . . .'

JIMMY. Oh yeah . . . 'His cries for help were answered when the
young man that he was chasing came back to assist him, a factor
that later contributed to the leniency of the sentence.' That's a
deadly word ain't it? Leniency.

LINDA. 'The judge said summing up that the defendant James
Brady was a nuisance and a danger to the public. He resisted
arrest and was constantly in trouble with the police. "The sooner
he grows up the better for all of us."'

JIMMY. Hey don't forget, 'The probation act was applied.'

LINDA. What did you do Jimmy, learn it off by heart or
somethin'?

JIMMY. The whole town has it off by heart. I'm famous sure.
They don't know now whether I should be crucified or ascended
into heaven. I have about twelve of those cuttings at home. Every
time Paddy rips one down I stick another up. Conway is
ragin' . . .

I don't know what you're lookin' at me like that for. I did it for
you.

LINDA (*baffled*). For me?

JIMMY. Yeah. I was skint. If I was goin' to take you somewhere I
needed some money fast didn't I? I mean I couldn't turn up with
no money again could I?

LINDA. And that's why you broke into the shop?

JIMMY. Ah I've been knockin' off that place for ages. It was a
cinch. In through the window and the money was always left in
the same drawer. The only thing was they had a trap set for me.
There was all this dye or ink or somethin' all over the money
and it stained all me hands and clothes. So when he picked me
up he knew straight away that I was the one.

LINDA. And that's when you took off up onto the roof?

JIMMY *nods*.

I mean you must have known that you couldn't get away? It was stupid.

JIMMY. Yeah I suppose it was.

LINDA. Why did you do it then?

JIMMY. I don't know. I just felt like it at the time.

He goes across to the cue stand.

LINDA. You just felt like it?

JIMMY. Yeah. It seemed like a good idea . . . (*He puts up the cue.*) at the time.

LINDA *shakes her head and smiles in disbelief. He smiles across at her.*

Look, I've always enjoyed knockin' off stuff. Ever since I was a young lad and I'd rob me Da's pockets while he was asleep in the chair. He'd have come in stocious drunk and gave me poor Ma a couple of belts and maybe broke the place up too into the bargain. Then he'd flop down into the armchair and demand his dinner. When he was asleep, snorin' his big head off, I'd rifle his coat pockets. He'd wake up dyin' and not a penny to his name.

LINDA. You'd rob your own Da?

JIMMY. Yeah. Why not? If somebody has somethin' I want I'll take it.

LINDA. What, anybody?

JIMMY. No, not anybody. Yeah though, anybody. Why not?

LINDA. Aw I can't believe that. What, even Tony yeh mean.

JIMMY. Yeah, if he had somethin' I wanted.

LINDA (*shakes her head*). I can't . . . I mean I know your brother Dick real well and he's terrible nice.

JIMMY. Yeah well Richard follows me Ma.

LINDA. And who do you follow?

JIMMY (*shrugs*). Naw I wouldn't rob Tony though. The fucker never has anythin' worth talkin' about anyway.

LINDA. But yeh would rob your Da?

JIMMY (*nods that he would*). If your Da was like mine you'd rob him too.

LINDA (*shakes her head in disbelief*). Your poor Ma must be addled between the two of you.

JIMMY *falls silent. He is sitting up on the pool table now, his legs dangling over the edge.*

JIMMY. I once caught them kissin' yeh know. Me Ma and Da I mean. I was only a little lad at the time. I ran out to tell Richard and when we got back me Da was singin' at the top of his voice and the two of them were waltzin' around the little kitchen. Me and Richard just stood starin' up at them. 'There they are now,' says me Da. 'James the Less and his brother Jude'. He had his good suit on him and a gleamin' white shirt and the smell of Brylcreem off him would nearly knock you down. Me Ma was breakin' her heart laughin' at the face of us, her own face lit up like a Christmas tree. I'm not coddin' you she looked absolutely . . . radiant. (*Pause.*) Richard says he doesn't remember that happenin' at all. Me Ma don't either. Maybe it was just a whatdoyoucallit . . . a mirage.

LINDA *has come closer to him now. She picks softly at his shirt, pulling at the loose threads.*

Richard kicked me Da out of the house yeh know when I was away with the F.C.A. that time.

LINDA. I never knew you were in the F.C.A.

JIMMY. Yeah I used to be. They threw me out of it. I got fed up of your man shoutin' at me. Whatshisname . . . yeh know your man lives up by you there . . . Brown! I told him to go and cop on himself. Anyway when I got home I found me Da stayin' down in that auld hostel. I felt terrible. He was just lyin' there, readin' a war book or somethin', a couple of those army blankets tossed across his feet. I wanted to burn the place down. I told him to get his things and come on home but he wouldn't. Well let's face it fellas like meself and me Da don't have a ghost of a chance do we? Like when I went looking for a job at your place. What did your man O'Brien ask me? What Brady are you then? Well that was me finished before I even started wasn't it?

LINDA. Aw he was probably only . . .

JIMMY. Yes he was yeah. He wrote me off straight away. Even if I had never been in trouble I was out. I wouldn't mind but he was knockin' off stuff all over the place himself. They found the generator in his car didn't they?

LINDA. Yeah.

JIMMY. And I heard they found a load of more stuff up in his garage – stuff belongin' to the firm. And he didn't even get the sack out of it did he?

LINDA. He's still down there anyway.

JIMMY shakes his head and smirks at the idea.

JIMMY. It's just as well I didn't get a job down there anyway. I'd never have been able to stick that Conway. I can't stomach that fella I'm not coddin' yeh. Did you know he's after talkin' Tony into gettin' married?

LINDA. To who? Not to that young one surely?

JIMMY. Yeah. She's up the pole sure. And now Conway is preachin' to him that the decent thing to do is to marry her.

LINDA. Well if it's his child . . .

JIMMY. Look Conway never stopped at him when Tony started goin' out with her first. Did you do this yet and did you do that yet? Badgerin' and jeerin' the chap and makin' a holy show of him in front of everyone. And now all of a sudden he's preachin' about what's right and what's wrong. All of a sudden she's a grand little girl . . . Tony don't want to marry her anyway.

LINDA. Poor Tony. He's real nice. (*She studies* JIMMY's *face.*) What would you do if you were in his shoes?

JIMMY. I'd run for the hills.

LINDA. Aw you wouldn't.

JIMMY. No not half wouldn't I.

LINDA *watches him carefully, trying to see if he is only joking.*

(*Earnestly.*) I would.

LINDA (*disappointed, turns away*). Let's get out of here Jimmy. This place is stinkin'.

JIMMY. We only just got here.

LINDA. I know but . . .

JIMMY (*going to her, putting his arms around her, kissing her gently*). What's wrong with yeh?

LINDA. Nothin'. I'd just prefer to be somewhere else that's all.

JIMMY. Yeah well we're not somewhere else are we? We're here.

LINDA. I know but I'd prefer to go someplace else.

JIMMY. Where?

LINDA. I don't know.

JIMMY. Do you want to go to the dance?

LINDA. How can we go to the dance when you're barred from the hall?

JIMMY. Yeah well you can go in on your own can't yeh? I don't mind.

LINDA. Look Jimmy if I'm goin' with a fella I'm goin' with him.

JIMMY. I know that. I just thought you liked dancin' that's all.

LINDA. I do like dancin'.

JIMMY. Well then?

LINDA. I'll just have to live without it won't I?

JIMMY *sighs and winces.*

What's wrong?

JIMMY. You'll have to live without goin' to the pictures too.

LINDA. Why, what did you do up there?

JIMMY. I asked the auld fella do be on the door how much would he charge to haunt a house? Did you ever see the face on him. He's like a ghost ain't he?

JIMMY *is laughing and so is* LINDA *in spite of herself.* JIMMY *kisses her, hugs her, wraps his arms around her.* LINDA *responds.* JIMMY *gradually caresses her all over, her hair, her neck. Eventually he tries to slip his hand up her jumper. She stops him.*

(*Whispers.*) What's wrong?

LINDA. I don't want you runnin' for the hills do I?

JIMMY. I said if I was in Tony's shoes I'd run for the hills. I'm not.

LINDA. You're in Jimmy Brady's shoes are yeh?

JIMMY. Yeah.

LINDA *considers this answer.*

Well they're me brother Richard's shoes actually but . . .

LINDA *smiles. She then takes the initiative and kisses him, running her fingers through his hair.*

Lights down.

ACT TWO

Scene One

The Club with TONY *standing over the pool table, setting up a game.* PADDY *is kneeling beside the stove, cleaning it out.* CONWAY *is sitting on the long bench reading the paper.*

CONWAY. Did yeh back anythin' Paddy?

PADDY. What? No. I put a few shillin's on a Flog the Horse alright but . . . I don't know what way he went. I didn't have time to . . .

CONWAY. He's down the field Paddy.

PADDY. Down is he?

CONWAY. Yeah. (*He gives it the thumbs down.*) Like a ton of bricks. (*He turns to another page.*) Well I was right about Stapler after anyway.

PADDY. What about him?

CONWAY. He's after movin' in with the queer one.

PADDY. What queer one?

CONWAY. The hairdresser I was tellin' yeh about.

PADDY. He's after leavin' the missus yeh mean?

CONWAY. Yeah.

TONY. Who, Stapler is? He never said nothin' to me in work about it then.

CONWAY. You don't think he's goin' to confide in a garsun like you do yeh? He moved out. Lock, stock and barrel. His Marty Robbins records and everything. That's why we haven't seen him lately. He's on a second honeymoon Paddy.

PADDY. God, and Stapler was married to a grand girl.

CONWAY. Well there y'are now Paddy.

JIMMY BRADY *comes out of the toilet buttoning his fly.*

TONY. Did you hear anything about that Jimmy?

JIMMY. What?

TONY. Conway says Stapler is after leavin' the missus. He's after movin' in with the queer one.

JIMMY. Yeah I heard somethin' about that alright. What's wrong with it Paddy? All the coal gone on yeh? The fairies must be usin' it all Paddy when you're not here.

TONY *smirks as* JIMMY *winks across to him.* PADDY *sighs as he slowly rises.*

TONY. The auld back at yeh Paddy?

PADDY. When you get to my age boy you'll realise that your back is the most important part of your body.

JIMMY. That's only because your front is wore out Paddy.

CONWAY. Stapler was always the same though lads yeh know. Even when he was a chap. He never half does anythin' yeh know? It's the whole hog or nothin' for Stapler.

PADDY. Sure how could he get out of it. His Da was the very axe same. Poor Denny. He was an awful case.

CONWAY. He did a bunk or somethin' didn't he?

PADDY. Yeah. He jumped ship in South America or somewhere. That's the last was ever heard tell of him. God I remember when he used to come home from sea with these great swanky suits on him and his hair slicked back that way man. He made us all want to run away to sea.

CONWAY. Did you know him well Paddy?

PADDY. I was reared right next door to him sure. Majestic Avenue.

CONWAY. Is that what they called it then? They've a different name on it now haven't they? What's this it is?

PADDY (*mostly to himself*). Little scutty houses with whitewashed walls – all flaky . . . and an outside lav. What am I talkin' about? Sure even the tap was outside the back door.

CONWAY. Dandy Street!

PADDY. Me poor Ma used to be blue with the cold traipsin' in and out for water. She reared twelve children in that house on her own. Eight hefty chaps all sleepin' in the one room. Upside down and sideways and skewways and I don't know what the hell way we slept at all.

CONWAY. You saw more dinner times than dinners I'd say Paddy, did yeh?

PADDY. What? Yeah. Off to school in the mornin's with no shoes on your feet. And you'd get no help or sympathy from anyone either. And then they try to tell me they were the good old days. The good old days me hat.

CONWAY. So the bould Stapler is followin' in his Da's footsteps then Paddy?

PADDY. What's that?

CONWAY. I say Stapler is a chip off the old block.

PADDY. Yeah. It looks like it alright.

JIMMY. But sure Stapler didn't run away.

CONWAY (*standing in the doorway*). What?

JIMMY. Stapler's not in South America. He's still here . . . in town.

CONWAY. Well he may as well be in South America as far as I'm concerned. Is the closet opened Paddy?

PADDY. Yeah. It's open in there.

CONWAY *goes into the back room.*

JIMMY. Hey Paddy that reminds me. You're supposed to throw open the table to us today.

PADDY. What?

JIMMY. Come on. Tony is gettin' married in the mornin'. We're entitled to free games for the rest of the day.

PADDY. What's he on about?

JIMMY. It's a tradition Paddy. When a fella is gettin' married . . .

PADDY. It's the first I heard of it then.

JIMMY. Yeah well it's a brand new tradition. Meself and Tony are the first to start it.

PADDY. You'll be lucky.

PADDY *disappears into the back room, coughing.* JIMMY *stands there and watches him go.*

JIMMY (*under his breath*). Go away yeh main auld bastard yeh . . .

TONY. You'll be gettin' us threw out of here boy.

JIMMY *chalks his cue, smirking.*

JIMMY (*circling the table*). Not at all.

PADDY *comes back out of the back room, climbing into his overcoat and fetching his scarf.*

Are yeh off Paddy?

PADDY. I'm only goin' down as far as the shop.

JIMMY. Do you know how to get there Paddy? Go out the door here and turn left right? – well go down the stairs first of course – anyway turn left and you'll see a laneway right opposite yeh. Don't bother goin' near there Paddy 'cause the shop is not up there.

PADDY *throws* JIMMY *a dirty look and continues on his way out the door.* TONY *cringes and backs away, trying to disassociate himself from* JIMMY's *behaviour.* JIMMY *shouts after* PADDY *at the top of his voice.*

Just follow your nose Paddy. Only wipe that big drop off the end of it first or you'll end up in South America along with Stapler's Da.

JIMMY *turns back to the game and takes his shot. When he notices that* TONY *is looking into the back room he steals an extra shot and lines up for yet a third one.* TONY *twigs it.*

TONY. Hey Jimmy what are you at there?

JIMMY. What?

TONY. It's my go.

JIMMY. What? Ha ha . . . Go on then. Come on, come on, let's get movin' here.

JIMMY *is all psyched up and raring to go. As* TONY *bends to take his shot* JIMMY *springs up behind him and rams the cue between his legs so that* TONY *is raised up and suspended in mid air.*

TONY (*in agony*). Aw come on Jimmy I didn't mess when you were firin'.

JIMMY. Who's the King of the Renegades Tony?

TONY. You are.

JIMMY (*lets him down*). Yeah well don't forget it.

TONY *caresses his groin.* JIMMY *paces about.*

Hey by the way Tony, what did Mary think of the wallpaperin' we done?

TONY. She said it's alright.

JIMMY. What?

TONY. She thought it was grand.

JIMMY. Did she spot the bad patch down behind the door?

TONY. Yeah she spotted that straight away.

JIMMY. Yeah well I hope yeh told her that you did that yourself . . .

TONY. The flat is startin' to take shape now though ain't it?

JIMMY. What? Yeah it's alright . . . Did the bed arrive yet?

TONY. No, not yet.

JIMMY. When is that supposed to come?

TONY. I don't know. I'll have to finish payin' for it first I suppose . . . The day after tomorrow I'd say.

JIMMY. You'll be alright then Tony. Awake every mornin' at the love and passionate hour of five past seven. Just roll over, put your arms around her and oh ha . . .

JIMMY *has come up beside* TONY. *He puts his arm around him and knocks him back onto the pool table, scattering the balls all over the place.* JIMMY *throws himself on top of* TONY, *climbing up on him, throwing his leg over him as* TONY *tries halfheartedly to fight him off.*

LINDA *comes in, catching* JIMMY *in this position.*

JIMMY. How are yeh?

He strolls across to the table and bends to take his shot. TONY *shies away, turning towards the glass panel.*

Hey where were you by the way?

LINDA (*furious*). Where was I? Where were you would be more like it.

JIMMY. Quarter to seven we said.

LINDA. Half seven.

JIMMY. Quarter to.

LINDA. Jimmy I told you I was workin' overtime tonight and you were supposed to meet me outside the factory at half past seven.

JIMMY. I was there. At quarter to seven like we said.

LINDA. Yes you were yeah. Pull the other one Jimmy.

JIMMY. Tony, where was I at quarter to seven tonight?

TONY (*who has not been listening, turning around startled*). What? Where? I don't know.

JIMMY. Was I outside the factory at quarter to seven tonight waitin' for her, yes or no?

TONY. Outside the factory? Oh yeah. You were, alright.

LINDA *throws* TONY *a dirty look.* TONY *is embarrassed and turns away from the row.*

LINDA. Jimmy I know where you were at quarter to seven tonight. You were here. And I know where you were this afternoon too.

JIMMY. Where?

LINDA. You were drinkin' down in the Shark.

JIMMY. Yeah well, I wasn't supposed to meet you this afternoon was I?

LINDA. I know you were with Maureen Carley.

JIMMY. Yeah Maureen was there.

LINDA. You were with her, drinkin' with her. You were seen.

JIMMY. Who saw me?

LINDA. Conway saw you. And he was only too glad to tell me about it in front of everyone. He said you left the bar with her.

JIMMY. Yeah well I couldn't stick listenin' to him yappin' any longer. I had to get out.

LINDA. And she had to go with you I suppose?

JIMMY. She was goin' home.

LINDA. You needn't think you're going to make an ejit out of me at all boy.

JIMMY. She was goin' home. She went one way and I went the other.

LINDA. The whole feckin' place was laughin' at me down there. They all thought it was very funny.

JIMMY. You can't blame me for that Linda.

LINDA (*sighs*). Anyway that's why I came down here tonight.

JIMMY. Why?

LINDA. Just in case you were laughin' at me too.

JIMMY. I'm not laughin'. Do you see me laughin'?

LINDA. Yeah well you might take me for a fool and I'm not. I know who you were with and what you were up to. Okay?

JIMMY *nods*.

So the best thing you can do now is to stay away from me in the future. I don't want to see you again. Right?

JIMMY. Hang on Linda . . .

LINDA. There's no hangin' on Jimmy. Every time we had a date you were either drunk or late or else you didn't bother to turn up at all.

JIMMY. There was only one other time, as far as I can remember, that I didn't turn up and that was the night . . .

LINDA. Look I don't care. I'm sick of yeh. I'm gettin' nothin' only hassle over yeh anyway.

JIMMY. From who?

LINDA. From me Ma and Da. From the girls at work. We can't go to the pictures, we can't go to a dance . . . You're bad news Jimmy.

JIMMY. Yeah well maybe I am bad news and all the rest of it but let's talk about it. I'll get me coat and we'll go somewhere.

LINDA. Where?

JIMMY. We'll go for a walk somewhere.

LINDA (*sarcastically*). A walk?

JIMMY. Look Linda, Tony is gettin' married in the mornin'. We're supposed to be goin' to the weddin'.

LINDA. Tony don't need me to get married. He don't need you either.

JIMMY. Hang on and I'll get me coat.

LINDA. Don't bother. I don't want to talk about it anyway.

JIMMY. Well I do.

LINDA. And I don't. That's not why I came down here. I never had to follow any fella in me life and I'm not goin' to start with you.

JIMMY. I know that.

JIMMY *moves in closer to her, glancing over his shoulder to make sure that* TONY *is not watching or listening. He tenderly caresses her face with the back of his hand and whispers.*

Give us a chance Linda will yeh?

LINDA (*sighs and grows a little tender*). There's no point Jimmy. You'll only end up soft-soapin' me. I'll go home tonight delighted with meself but tomorrow or the next day I'll wake up to find we're back where we started . . . Conway's right about you Jimmy, you're not goin' to change.

The door opens behind them and in comes PADDY *carrying a toilet roll and a bottle of Dettol. He looks at the girl and frowns, condemning her presence.* JIMMY *pulls away from* LINDA *at the sight of* PADDY. TONY *shuffles uneasily until* PADDY *has coughed his way into the back room.* LINDA *is sickened by the sight of* PADDY *and by the reaction of the two boys.*

LINDA. Go back to your game will yeh before Tony has a heart attack there.

TONY *winces as* LINDA *storms out the door.* JIMMY *makes a move to follow her, gets as far as the door, stops, hangs his head and sighs.* TONY *doesn't know what to do or say.* JIMMY *eventually closes the door and comes back to the table. He chalks his cue.* TONY *is hesitant, watching the door, thinking to himself that* JIMMY *should go after her.*

JIMMY. Come on Tony will yeh, it's your go.

TONY *stoops to fire.*

Do you want to go down to the Shark after this game or what?

TONY. No I can't. I've to go and meet Mary.

JIMMY (*raging*). What for?

TONY. We've to go and check that the hotel is alright.

JIMMY. How long will yeh be?

TONY. About an hour I'd say. I'll meet you down there sure.

JIMMY *exhales a long, complaining sigh, turning his back on* TONY, *gazing angrily into the back room. We catch a glimpse of* CONWAY *staring out at him.*

It's your shot Jimmy.

JIMMY *turns slowly, steps up to the table and with a furious sweep of his hand he scoops all the remaining balls down into the pockets, ending the game prematurely.* TONY *scratches himself and fidgets. Eventually he goes over and gets his coat, puts it on and walks towards the front door.*

I'll see yeh down in the Shark then Jimmy, in about an hour or so. All the lads from work are probably down there by now anyway.

TONY *waits for a reply but* JIMMY *doesn't respond.* TONY *skulks out the door leaving* JIMMY *alone in the club with the sound of laughter escaping from the back room.*

Scene Two

The Club a few hours later. CONWAY *is playing the one-armed bandit.* PADDY *enters from the toilet doorway carrying a bucket of coal. Dean Martin is singing 'King of the Road' on the jukebox, the last few bars of it.*

CONWAY. Well the bold Jimmy Brady was at it again Paddy.

PADDY. What's that?

CONWAY. Jimmy Brady.

PADDY. What about him?

CONWAY. I say he was boxin' down the Shark tonight. So I heard anyway.

PADDY. Who was tellin' yeh this?

CONWAY. One of the young lads was sayin' it here. It seems he bursted Wally the barman with a headbutt.

PADDY (*sighs*). That's a right cur that fella is.

CONWAY. Oh now I believe it was scandalous altogether. The big lad came out over the counter after him and everything – tables and drinks spilt all over the place.

PADDY *moves towards the back room.*

Only Stapler managed to get him out, they were sayin' that the big lad would have killed him.

PADDY. What's wrong with that young fella at all eh?

CONWAY. He's a bad 'erb Paddy, that's what's wrong with him.

PADDY. He's the same as his Da so. Jaysus that coileain gave that poor woman an awful life so he did.

CONWAY. Yeah well he won't do it no more then Paddy, 'cause Dick – the other brother – shagged him out of the house altogether. I believe he's stayin' down in that auld hostel for the homeless now.

PADDY (*surprised*). Who? Jimmy's Da is stayin' down in the hostel now is he?

CONWAY. Yeah. Sure he hasn't been livin' at home this five or six weeks now. I'd say that woman is not sorry to see the back of him either Paddy would you?

PADDY (*sighs*). No God I remember when the two of them were only courtin'. She's was dyin' alive about that fella. I often saw them up in the Town Hall and they waltzin' the legs off one another. They were grand dancers too. He used to be all done up like a dog's dinner I'm not coddin' yeh – great suits on him and all. And she'd be smilin' up into his face all the time. To look at her you'd swear she had just swallowed a handful of stars. Jaysus she was a lovely girl, so she was.

CONWAY. Yeah but that was many moons ago though Paddy.

PADDY. What's that?

CONWAY. I say that was a long time ago.

PADDY. Yeah, it was a long time ago alright.

PADDY *disappears into the back room.* CONWAY *goes back to the one-armed bandit. Enter* STAPLER *just as* PADDY *is coming back out, wiping his hands in his coat.*

STAPLER (*ignoring* CONWAY). Was Jimmy or Tony in Paddy?

PADDY. No they weren't Stapler. They were in here a few hours ago alright but I haven't seen them since. Conway was sayin' that Jimmy Brady was fightin' down in the Shark.

STAPLER. Yeah he was. There was murders down there.

CONWAY. How is Wally? Is he badly hurt?

STAPLER. Naw. A couple of stitches I'd say. But some of the lads were tellin' me that Jimmy went home after the row and got his brother's shotgun – Dick's – and he tried to hold up that little huckster's shop on the corner here. Whatdoyoucallit . . .

PADDY. Flynn's?

STAPLER. Yeah Flynn's. He had this great nylon stocking pulled down over his face but sure the young one recognised him.

PADDY (*disgusted*). A shotgun though to rob a little huckster's shop. Lord God Almighty tonight what kind of a . . .

CONWAY. So they nabbed him did they?

STAPLER. No they didn't. He took off sure. There's cops swarmin' all over the place now lookin' for him. There's some of them armed too I believe.

CONWAY. And was Tony implicated in all this?

STAPLER. I don't think so. Tony wasn't down in the Shark anyway when the row broke out. It was just Jimmy on his own I think knocked off the shop.

PADDY. Oh when it comes to being a cannatt that fella don't need any help.

CONWAY. Do yeh know what I'd do with that lad if I had him?

STAPLER. But sure what can yeh do Conway? The chap is wild. That's all's wrong with him.

CONWAY. Wild! I'd wild him.

STAPLER. I mean yeh can't blame young fellas for goin' off the rails either can yeh?

CONWAY. How do yeh mean Stapler?

STAPLER. Well let's face it, if a young lad takes a good look around him what do he see? He sees a crowd of big shots and hob-nobbers grabbin' and takin' all before them. But as soon as a young lad knocks off a few bob out of a poor box or somewhere they're all down on him like a ton of bricks. Like your man down in the factory – O'Brien – knocking off stuff right, left and centre, caught red-handed too. What happened to him? Nothin'. Nothin' happened to him.

CONWAY. That's beside the point Stapler. Yeh can't go around headbutting fellas every time you feel it.

STAPLER. Aw I know that. I'm not sayin' that . . .

CONWAY. Look you're goin' around now lookin' all over the place for Jimmy Brady. What's goin' to happen when you find him? Do yeh think he's goin' to thank yeh? Do yeh think he's goin' to throw his arms around yeh or somethin'? I mean what are yeh goin' to do Stapler? What are yeh goin' to say?

STAPLER. I don't know. Try to get that gun off of him for a start before he does somethin' drastic. Maybe try talk a bit of sense into him.

CONWAY. Yeah, well away with yeh. Rather you than me. As far as I'm concerned Jimmy Brady is a thorn in the side of this town and the sooner he gets his comeuppance the better.

CONWAY *goes to the one-armed bandit, turning his back on* STAPLER.

STAPLER. The thing is I'm after tryin' everywhere I can think of.

CONWAY. Where did you look for him anyway?

STAPLER. All over the place. I tried the back room of Bryne's Café. I checked out the slaughterhouse yard too – remember Paddy he used to work up in the slaughterhouse one time – I even climbed up into his granda's auld pigeon loft. Wherever there was a shadow I looked for him.

PADDY (*stepping forward*). Did yeh look down the back of the station?

STAPLER. The goods yard yeh mean?

PADDY. Yeah. I know he used to hang around there a lot. I often caught a glimpse of him in there when I'd be goin' home at night.

STAPLER. No I never thought of trying there Paddy. (*Pause.*) Sure if you hear anything give us a shout will yeh?

PADDY. Yeah right Stapler. But sure they've probably nabbed him by now anyway.

STAPLER (*from the doorway*). Oh more than likely. (*Pause.*) Good luck lads.

PADDY. All the best.

STAPLER *leaves.* CONWAY *refuses to acknowledge him at all and lets him go without uttering a word or even glancing in his direction.* PADDY *is standing there, staring into space.* CONWAY *comes up behind him.*

CONWAY. Did yeh hear Stapler? He's goin' to talk a bit of sense into Jimmy Brady. He'd want to get a bit of sense himself first.

CONWAY *laughs and goes into the back room to fetch his coat. He comes back out climbing into it. The rustle causes* PADDY *to turn and look at him.*

PADDY. Are yeh off?

CONWAY. Yeah, I'm goin' to take a bit of a stroll around and see what's happenin'. Where did Stapler say the cops were?

PADDY. I don't know.

CONWAY. I'll follow the crowds Paddy. Listen if I were you I'd shut up shop early tonight because if he's on the rampage he's bound to head for here.

PADDY (*thinks about it*). Yeah.

CONWAY. Well you'll definitely have the cops on yeh one way or another.

PADDY. Yeah.

CONWAY (*moves to the door, stopping in the doorway*). There's never a dull moment either is there Paddy?

He leaves. PADDY *stands there pondering on what to do. Then he goes into the back room, switches out the light and locks the door. He then gets a chair and turns off the street lights. After that he puts the cues back in place.* SWAN *comes in.* PADDY *is startled.*

SWAN (*looking all around*). Anybody about Paddy?

PADDY. No.

SWAN. No?

SWAN *goes snooping around – into the toilet, peering in through the glass panel, trying the door to the back room, nodding for* PADDY *to open it.*

PADDY. There's no one in there.

SWAN. Open up.

PADDY *opens up.* SWAN *goes stealthily in.*

Where's the light switch?

PADDY. Just above your head there. No on your right.

The light comes on and we catch a glimpse of SWAN *looking around in there. He comes back out.*

SWAN. Yeah. It's very quiet isn't it?

PADDY. Yeah. Sure there's nothin' doing'.

SWAN. Are yeh closing up or what Paddy?

PADDY. Yeah.

SWAN. I was just passing by when I saw your lights goin' out. I thought there was somethin' up.

PADDY. Aw no, there's nothin' the matter or anythin' like that.

SWAN. Mmn . . . Tell me Paddy, was Jimmy Brady in here tonight?

PADDY. No. He was in here earlier on alright. This evenin' like.

SWAN. Yeah I know he was in here this evenin' but was he in here tonight?

PADDY. He wasn't, no.

SWAN *studies the old man's face for a lie or the least hint of one.*

SWAN. He wasn't?

PADDY. No.

SWAN (*drumming his fingers on the edge of the pool table*). Yes begor . . . He's on the warpath. You heard that I suppose did you?

PADDY. I heard somethin' about that alright.

SWAN. Yeah. Our brave Jimmy shattered a squad car window with a blast from a shotgun no less. It's the luck of God no one was in it at the time. He then hit a young guard with the butt of the

gun. I'd be very surprised now if the chap's jaw is not broken.
This all happened after he caused ructions down in the Shark
and tried to hold up a shop.

All the time SWAN *is searching* PADDY's *face for some form of*
expression or opinion — sympathy or delight — just a sign to show which
side the old man is on. PADDY *is unmoved.*

He's already put two people in hospital and the night is young
yet.

PADDY *remains dead-pan much to* SWAN's *chagrin.* SWAN *looks*
around at the dinginess of the club, his dislike and distaste for the place
showing in his face.

What in the name of God do anyone in his right mind see in this
place at all? It'd put years on me now this place would. Do you
not think it's an awful waste of a lifetime Paddy, hanging around
a kip like this? Sure you'd want to be a mental pygmy to stick
this place day in and day out. What?

PADDY *just shrugs.*

You must have no respect for yourself Paddy. That's all I can
say. You must have no respect for yourself. You can't have.
You've been working here now as long as I can remember and I
came to town over fourteen years ago. And in all that time you
never even tried to . . . I can't understand that Paddy. Can you
understand it yourself?

PADDY. Ah sure, we all can't be Sergeant Majors.

SWAN. Now you listen to me. If Jimmy Brady comes in here you
get in touch with me. Do you hear me now?

PADDY *nods.*

If you lay eyes on him, either tonight or tomorrow or whenever,
you call me straight away. And I won't take any feeble excuses
from you either Paddy, like I forgot or I never thought. You
were always good at forgettin' when it was convenient. Well not
this time Paddy. This time don't forget. Because I'm gettin' sick
and tired of this little den of rogues you're runnin' here boy.
Yeh see I don't forget Paddy. I remember . . . I remember all the
small town hard cases and corner boys I've chased and caught
through the years. I remember the ones that gave me the slip
too. They're the ones that stick out in my mind most of all. I'd
come in here to find them all lookin' as innocent as you please

and I'd have to let it go at that. What's this they used to call this place then Paddy? The Rio Grande? Ha Ha . . . Yes. The Rio Grande (*He pronounces 'Grande' differently the second time.*) . . . but not this time Paddy 'cause I want to know how you're fixed boy. I want to know which side you're on. (*He stares at the old man for ages just to drive his point home. He makes to leave, stops and turns, pointing his thumb towards the toilet.*) By the way, did you know you've a broken window in the lav, there?

PADDY. What? Oh yeah, I know that. There's an auld pane missin'.

SWAN. Well I suggest you get it fixed. It's no use calling me in three or four months time to tell me the place has been broken into, because if I find that window still like that I'll just turn around and tell yeh that you asked for it.

SWAN *leaves.*

Lights down.

Scene Three

The Club. Lights come up on JIMMY *who is sitting in a moody half light. He is ruffled-looking and his hand is bleeding. The glass panel behind him is smashed, with 'Jimmy' scrawled in chalk on the door.* TONY *enters through the front door which has been left ajar.*

TONY. Jimmy, Jimmy, where are yeh?

JIMMY. I'm over here. Come in and close the door after yeh.

TONY (*closing the door gently*). What did yeh leave it open like that for? I could have been anybody. (*The sight of the smashed glass panel stops* TONY *in his tracks.*) What happened here? Aw Jaysus Jimmy there was no need to go and do that . . .

JIMMY. Give it a rest will yeh.

TONY *looks down at* JIMMY *in disgust.*

What are you lookin' at me like that for? You'd think I was after pissin' on a shrine or somethin' the way you're goin' on. That's only a room in there Tony. It's just a room.

TONY *hangs his head, disappointed that* JIMMY *has abused the back room.* JIMMY *eyes his woebegone friend.*

Look if you're worried about gettin' the blame for this don't. I'll tell them you had nothin' to do with it. Okay?

TONY. That doesn't matter.

JIMMY. Yes it does matter. When I get out I expect you to be a staunch member here with your own key and everything. Sure you've already got the ingredients to be a miniature Conway. Money in the Credit Union and a set of bicycle clips now and you'll be away with it.

TONY. There's nothin' wrong with Conway, Jimmy, he's alright.

JIMMY. Oh I know he's alright. You can bet your sweet life on that. The Creep.

TONY. So he's a creep and you're a fuckin' ejit. What's the difference?

JIMMY. None I suppose. But if I had a choice I'd prefer to be an ejit than a creep.

TONY. Why?

JIMMY. I don't know. I just would.

TONY (sighs). Look what do you want to do Jimmy?

JIMMY. What? I don't know.

TONY. Well you'd better make up your mind. I'm gettin' married in the mornin' don't forget.

JIMMY. I don't think so Tony. I think I just got you a reprieve.

TONY. What are you talkin' about?

JIMMY. Listen I want you to do me a favour. I want you to go up to the barracks and tell them where to find me.

TONY (flabbergasted). Haw? What do you think I am, a squealer or somethin'? I couldn't do that . . .

JIMMY. Look I'm askin' you to go . . . as a favour. I don't want them burstin' in here after me like they were the Sweeney or somethin'.

TONY paces up and down nervously, shaking his head.

TONY. You're landin' me right in the middle of it all. Supposin' Swan decides to hold on to me for the night too. What if one of those bastards feels like takin' it out on me? They might try and implicate me just because I was with you earlier on tonight . . .

JIMMY *is sitting there biting his nails, a frightened, hunted look in his eyes.* TONY *sees that* JIMMY *is afraid and stops talking.* TONY *sighs and there is a long silence while* TONY *thinks it over.*

What do you want me to say?

JIMMY. Tell them where I am. Tell them the door will be wide open and the lights full on. And don't forget to say that I'm unarmed.

TONY. The door will be wide open and the lights full on. And he's unarmed.

JIMMY. Yeah. Go to Swan himself.

TONY. Where is the gun anyway?

JIMMY. Tell them you don't know where it is.

TONY. What? Now they're goin' to want to know where that gun is.

JIMMY. That's their hard luck.

TONY. Aw come on Jimmy I'm supposed to be gettin' married in the mornin'. I don't fancy gettin' the ears boxed off me half the night over you. What's the point anyway?

JIMMY. The point is you never know when you might need a gun. You might be glad of it one day to blow your brains out.

TONY. What are you on about? Gettin' me a reprieve. And me blowing me brains out. Anyone would think that it was me who was in trouble or somethin'. Jimmy you're the one that's goin' up the river not me.

JIMMY. Never mind about that. I know well enough where I'm goin'. But you've been shanghai'd in your sleep Tony. You're on a slow boat to China or somewhere boy and yeh don't even realise it.

TONY (*angry and hurt*). At least I never went berserk over a girl anyway.

JIMMY. This has nothin' to do with her.

TONY. Oh yeah? Pull the other one Jimmy. Linda gave you the shove and you went berserk. Admit it.

JIMMY. She didn't give me the shove. We had a bit of a row that's all.

TONY. Oh yeah? Well then why don't yeh get her to do your dirty
work for yeh. Why don't you ask her to go up and see Swan . . .
No, you won't do that will yeh? 'Cause yeh have the auld gom
here. Well you needn't think now for one minute that I'm goin'
up there until I know exactly where that gun is 'cause I'm not.

JIMMY *shakes his head and smiles.* TONY *becomes furious and moves
in closer to* JIMMY.

What's so funny Jimmy?

JIMMY. You. You'd give it all up just like that wouldn't yeh?
You'd hand it to them on a plate. Well not me. I want to see
them runnin' around, like blue arsed flies. And when I'm up in
that courtroom and somebody mentions a gun I'll say, 'Gun?
What gun? I don't see no gun.'

TONY. And what about the rest of us? What about me?

JIMMY. What about yeh?

TONY. They're goin' to assume that I know where it is. That you
told me.

JIMMY *just shrugs.*

You're a bad bastard you are.

JIMMY. Yeah that's right Tony. I'm a bad bastard. Where has
being a good boy ever got you?

TONY. The one night I ever asked yeh not to start anythin'. The
one night . . .

JIMMY. Yeah alright Tony. So what do you want me to do now?
Get down on me knees and kiss somebody's arse or somethin',
just because you're afraid to take a couple of clips in the ear?
Look if you don't want to do what I asked you to do, get the
fuck out of me sight.

TONY (*desperately*). I'm supposed to be gettin' married in the
mornin'.

JIMMY (*dismissive*). Go and fuck off away from me will yeh.

JIMMY *turns away from him.* TONY *stays where he is.* JIMMY *turns
back and shoves* TONY *away from him.*

Go on, get out of me sight before yeh make me vomit.

TONY (*brushing* JIMMY'*s hand aside*). Don't push Jimmy.

JIMMY (*pushing him again*). Why?

TONY. I'm warnin' yeh Jimmy, don't start.

> JIMMY *shoves* TONY *yet again.* TONY *loses his head and goes for him. There is a brawl with the two boys stumbling over the pool table and onto the floor. They punch one another and wrestle until* JIMMY *gets the better of* TONY. *He stands over the bleeding boy in a defiant stance.*

JIMMY. Nobody's goin' to wrap me up in a nice neat little parcel. I'm not goin' to make it handy for you to forget about me – not you, not me Ma nor me Da, not Swan, nobody.

> JIMMY *picks up a cue and holds it above his head.* TONY *cowers away from it.* JIMMY *turns and storms at the door to the back room and begins kicking it and hunching it with his shoulder. Eventually, as* TONY *gazes on in awe and disgust,* JIMMY *manages to break in, falling into the back room. We hear him wrecking the place in there, pulling down cupboards, kicking over chairs, scattering balls and breaking an out-of-sight window. When* JIMMY *appears in the doorway he has a frenzied look about him.*

Tell them Jimmy Brady done it. The same Jimmy Brady that's scrawled all over this town. Jimmy Brady who bursted that big bully of a bouncer with a headbutt when everyone else was afraid of their livin' lives of him. The same Jimmy Brady that led Detective Garda Swan twice around the houses and back again . . . Yeh see that's the difference between me and Conway. He tiptoes around. I'm screamin'. Me and Stapler are screamin'. So if you want to join the livin' dead then go ahead and do it by all means Tony but don't expect me to wink at your gravediggers. Conway . . . the big he-man with no bell on his bike. I hates him I'm not coddin' yeh I do.

TONY (*tearful*). It's not Conway's fault you're up to your ears in shit Jimmy. It's not my fault you fell out with your man in the bar. You can't blame Paddy for . . .

JIMMY. Alright. It's not Conway's fault, it's not your fault, it's not Paddy's . . . Who's fault is it then Tony? Mine? Tell me who's to blame will yeh til I tear his friggin' head off.

TONY (*sighs, stalls and comes closer to* JIMMY, *his voice taking on a more tender edge*). I don't know who's to blame. Maybe it's nobody's fault. Maybe that's just the way it is.

JIMMY. Yeah right, it's nobody's fault. (JIMMY *plonks himself down hopelessly on the bench.*) It's nobody's fault. Everyone's to blame.

There is a long painful silence. JIMMY *lights up a cigarette and drags on it.* TONY *shuffles nervously across to the back room, eyeing the devastation, heartbroken.* JIMMY *looks up at him.*

Go ahead in Tony. Go on, be a man.

TONY *turns his back on the room, bowing his head in sadness.*

What's wrong with yeh Tony? I thought you were dyin' to get in there. I thought you'd be mad to play on the big snooker table or to try out one of the poker chairs. What's the matter with yeh? Are you afraid that the lads are like the three bears or somethin', that they'll come back and catch yeh?

JIMMY *smiles sadly as he watches* TONY's *bent figure. Suddenly there is a noise off stage and the two boys smart to alertness, the two of them looking towards one another for confirmation,* JIMMY *jumping to his feet and getting ready to make a break for it. When* STAPLER *comes out of the toilet door, brushing himself down, the two boys sigh with relief.*

Stapler yeh frightened the life out of me.

STAPLER *gestures to them to keep their voices down as he tiptoes across to one of the shutters and peeps out through a crack.*

What's up?

STAPLER. There's cops swarmin' all over the place lookin' for you. That's what's up.

JIMMY (*terrified*). Are they comin' up here Stapler?

STAPLER (*calmly walking over towards the back room to view the damage*). What happened here?

TONY *eyes the floor in shame.* STAPLER's *eyes go from* TONY *to* JIMMY.

JIMMY. Me hand slipped, Stapler.

STAPLER *thinks about it and shrugs it off as unimportant.*

Hey by the way Stapler, how did you know how to get in here? (*He eyes* TONY *suspiciously.*)

TONY. I don't know what you're lookin' at me for Jimmy. I didn't tell him.

STAPLER. That window has been like that this fifteen years. Why, did you think you were the first to discover it or somethin'? (*He laughs and shakes his head in amusement.*) So what's the plan Jimmy?

JIMMY. Plan? What plan? I've no plan.

TONY. He wants me to go to the barracks and tell them where to find him.

STAPLER. Aw have a heart Jimmy, the chap is gettin' married in the mornin'.

JIMMY. So? Look all I'm askin' him to do is . . .

STAPLER. Yeah well that's not on at all.

TONY. I wouldn't mind going up but he won't even tell me where the gun is.

STAPLER. Don't worry about that Tony. That information can be bet out of him.

JIMMY (*defiantly*). Who's goin' to bate it out of me Stapler?

STAPLER *throws the boy a dirty look.*

STAPLER. Look I'll go up to the barracks for yeh alright. Now what do you want me to say?

JIMMY *is surprised.*

JIMMY. Just tell them the door will be wide open and the lights on. And don't forget to say that I'm unarmed. See Swan himself.

STAPLER *nods that he understands.*

STAPLER. You go up and tell Jimmy's Ma where he is Tony . . . when he's picked up I mean.

TONY. Yeah alright.

STAPLER. This'll break that woman's heart, yeh know that boy, don't yeh?

JIMMY. You can't break what's already broken Stapler. Anyway she won't be surprised. She always said I'd be a heart breaker when I grew up. A bit like yourself yeh know.

STAPLER. Breakin' hearts is not exactly my favourite pastime Jimmy.

JIMMY. Yeh could have fooled me then. I'll tell yeh one thing Stapler the boys are all ragin' with you here. They're all black out with yeh boy.

STAPLER. What?

JIMMY. Conway and all. They're disgusted with yeh.

STAPLER (*sarcastically*). I'm worried about them now!

JIMMY. What?

STAPLER. I don't give a shit about them.

JIMMY. How come we don't see yeh in here no more then?

STAPLER. What do yeh mean?

JIMMY. If yeh don't give a shit about them, why don't you come up to the club no more? You used to be in here all the time.

STAPLER. Look Jimmy, I don't have to answer to no one. Stapler goes his own way. Always has.

JIMMY. All the same though Stapler you go too far. Conway is very disappointed in you. Leavin' your missus like that without askin' for his permission . . .

STAPLER *goes to say something but changes his mind.*

STAPLER (*sighs*). Now you listen to me boy, if I go up here to the barracks for you I don't want you pullin' any fast stuff.

JIMMY. What do yeh mean?

STAPLER. I mean none of this Jesse James lark running across roofs and all the rest of it.

JIMMY *finds this amusing.*

I'm serious Jimmy. When the cops come down you be here . . . waitin'.

JIMMY. Do yeh hear Stapler? Givin' orders all over the place.

STAPLER. I'm tellin' yeh now. I'm puttin' me neck on the line for you boy and you'd better not let me down.

JIMMY. Yeah alright Stapler I know you're a bit of a whore master and all goin' around but I'm not one of your . . .

STAPLER *pounces on* JIMMY, *giving him a back-handed slap in the face.* STAPLER *grabs him by the hair and the lapel and pins him up against the pool table.*

STAPLER. I came down here to give you a hand boy and I don't fancy gettin' hit in the solar plexus every time I open me mouth. Right?

JIMMY. Alright Stapler, I was only messin'.

STAPLER *lets him go and steps back.*

STAPLER. I'm not exactly doin' meself any favours comin' down here Jimmy. There's no future for me in sidin' with you . . . You'd want to cop on to yourself boy.

JIMMY *fixes his attire.* TONY *looks uneasy.* STAPLER *calms himself down and goes across to the shutter to look out through the crack again.*

You make sure you're gone out of here before the cops arrive Tony. Do yeh hear me?

TONY. Yeah.

STAPLER. Now come on and shut this front door after me.

TONY *and* STAPLER *head towards the front door,* STAPLER *stopping halfway to face* JIMMY.

Most of us wage war on the wrong people Jimmy. I do it meself all the time. But you beat the bun altogether you do.

JIMMY. How's that?

STAPLER. You wage war on everybody.

JIMMY *doesn't know what to say.* STAPLER *sighs and turns away, heading towards the door.* TONY *opens it for him.* STAPLER *tosses his hair affectionately.*

I'll see yeh in the mornin' Tony.

TONY. Yeah right Stapler.

STAPLER. Take it easy Jimmy.

JIMMY. Yeah, I'll see yeh Stapler.

STAPLER *leaves. Pause.*

Give us a fag Tony will yeh?

TONY *takes out a packet of fags, takes one for himself and throws the packet across to* JIMMY. JIMMY *takes one out and offers the packet back to* TONY.

TONY. Sure you'd better hang on to them.

JIMMY. It's alright Tony. There's no point anyway. The bastards will only take them off me.

TONY *reluctantly takes the cigarettes back and pockets them. They light up and puff.*

This time tomorrow Tony I'll be . . . (JIMMY *runs a finger knife-like across his throat.*)

TONY. That makes two of us. (*The two boys give a little fey laugh.*)

JIMMY. Hey for a minute there I thought sure Stapler was goin' to burst me did you?

TONY. Yeah. He was queer mad, boy wasn't he?

JIMMY (*smiles about it*). He was right about one thing though.

TONY. What's that?

JIMMY. Me Ma'll go mad about this.

TONY. What'll your Da say?

JIMMY. I don't know. Throw a few fucks into me I suppose . . . It's me Ma I'm really worried about. She never says anythin' yeh know. But you can see the torment in her eyes if you look close. She never says a word. She just sort of broods. (*Pause.*) I'm not worried about me Da at all. But sure maybe this'll get them talkin' again if nothing else. It'd be gas wouldn't it?

TONY. What?

JIMMY. Did I ever tell yeh about the time I caught the two of them kissin'?

TONY (*embarrassed*). Yeah, yeh said somethin' about that alright.

JIMMY. I told you about that did I? Singin' at the top of his voice he was and the pair of them waltzin' around the little kitchen and me poor Ma lookin' like she hadn't a care in the world. 'There they are now,' says me Da. 'James the Less and his brother Jude.' That's a deadly name ain't it? James the Less.

TONY. Yeah. Who is he anyway?

JIMMY. I haven't a clue. (*Silence.*) You'd better be goin' soon Tony. They'll be arrivin' any minute now.

TONY. Yeah.

JIMMY. I'm goin' to tell yeh one thing boy, you've a fair shiner comin' up too. Mary'll go mad when she sees that.

TONY. What? Have I? (*He feels his swollen eye.*) I have too, yeh bastard yeh.

JIMMY *laughs. They fall silent.* TONY *goes across and takes another heartbroken look at the back room.* JIMMY *watches him.* TONY *makes a move to leave.*

I'll see yeh Jimmy.

JIMMY. Yeah, I'll see yeh Tony . . . Good luck tomorrow.

TONY. Thanks. (*He strides sadly towards the front door.*)

JIMMY. Hey Tony.

TONY (*from the doorway*). What? (*Pause.*)

JIMMY. Aw nothin'. It's alright. Go ahead.

The two boys stare at one another. Finally TONY *breaks away and leaves* JIMMY *alone in the moody half-light of the club.* JIMMY *goes across and puts some money in the jukebox. He plays a record and squats down beside the jukebox and lights another cigarette.*

Lights down.

POOR BEAST
IN THE RAIN

Poor Beast in the Rain was produced for television by Initial Film and Television and first screened on BBC-2 in summer 1993 as part of *The Wexford Trilogy*. The cast was as follows:

EILEEN	Dervla Kirwan
DANGER	Liam Cunningham
GEORGIE	Gary Lydon
JOE	Des McAleer
MOLLY	Ingrid Craigie
STEVEN	Michael O'Hagan

Directed by Stuart Burge, produced by Emma Burge and designed by Christine Edzard at the Sands Films studios in Rotherhithe.

Poor Beast in the Rain was first performed in London at the Bush Theatre, on 8 November 1989. The cast was as follows:

EILEEN	Catherine Cusack
DANGER	George Irving
GEORGIE	Gary Lydon
JOE	Des McAleer
MOLLY	Dearbhla Molloy
STEVEN	Denis Quilligan

Directed by Robin Lefevre
Designed by Andrew Wood
Lighting by Tina MacHugh

Characters

EILEEN
GEORGIE
JOE
STEVEN
MOLLY
DANGER DOYLE

The play is set in Wexford, a small town in Ireland. It has a time span of one week-end, the week-end leading up to the All Ireland Final. Scene One takes place on Friday evening. Scenes Two and Three on Saturday Morning. Act Two, Scene One takes place on Sunday night.

The play is set in an old fashioned betting shop. Stage left a counter runs into a wooden partition which is panelled here and there with frosted glass. A bench runs along the back wall of the shop. Stage right a few steps lead up into a little anteroom which has a couple of chairs and a table. There are three doors – one is the main front door and is situated stage left beside the partition. The second door is positioned behind the counter and seems to lead to an office. The third door is situated at the back of the anteroom, leading to a toilet and store room. There are two windows – one is a small curtained window behind the counter. The other is a big bay window in the anteroom. The counter is lined with all the usual stuff that can be found in a betting shop of this sort – pads and pencils and skewered dockets etc. Newspapers dot the walls. A speaker is mounted on the wall just above the bench.

ACT ONE

Scene One

Lights up on the betting shop. GEORGIE *is sitting on the wooden bench.* JOE *is sitting at the table, a spread-out newspaper in front of him.* EILEEN *is standing behind the counter. They are all listening to a race that is coming from a speaker on the wall.*

SPEAKER. And we're coming to the last furlong now and it's Dandy Boy, Elephant's Memory, Kissing Cousin, The Loafer and Napper Tandy all branching away from the rest of the field. And Elephant's Memory makes his move, cutting out on to the outside and Dandy Boy takes up the challenge and they're neck and neck now as The Loafer and Kissing Cousin battle it out behind for third place. But Elephant's Memory is inching forward and for my money it's going to be Elephant's Memory. It's got to be Elephant's Memory. Yes, winner alright. Elephant's Memory, Dandy Boy and The Loafer just shading it over Kissing Cousin for third with the favourite Napper Tandy well down the field.

EILEEN *writes in the winners on the result sheet behind the counter as* GEORGIE *palms a crinkled docket away.*

EILEEN. Hard luck Georgie.

GEORGIE. That's the story of my life.

EILEEN. Ah well, yeh nearly won.

GEORGIE. Yeah. But yeh know what they say about only nearly doin' somethin' though Eileen don't yeh?

EILEEN. No, what?

GEORGIE. Nearly never reaches.

EILEEN. Yeh got a good run for your money all the same.

GEORGIE. Yeah, I suppose I did.

SPEAKER. The starting price at Kempton. Elephant's Memory two-to-one. Dandy Boy eleven-to-two. The Loafer eight-to-one.

Eighteen ran and the dual forecast was twenty seventy. Off five fifteen.

EILEEN *writes in the starting price on the result sheet and then she comes out from behind the counter to mark off the results on the sheet above the bench.*

GEORGIE. Hey Eileen, why don't yeh come up to Dublin with us tomorrow?

EILEEN. What?

GEORGIE. I say why don't yeh come up to the match with us? I'll get yeh a ticket.

EILEEN. Ah, I don't think so Georgie.

GEORGIE. Why not?

EILEEN. I'd look well now.

GEORGIE. But sure you won't be the only girl there yeh know. Some of the women out of the factory are comin' too. Anyway Eileen you'll be browned off hangin' around here because this place is goin' to be deserted over the weekend. Dogs and cats and all'll be gone boy.

EILEEN. Good. I'm lookin' forward to a bit of peace and quiet.

EILEEN *sighs as she works, sorting through a skewer of dockets.* GEORGIE *is over at the counter now.*

GEORGIE. Under pressure?

EILEEN. Yeah . . . I'm fed up of this place to tell yeh nothin' but the truth . . . Did yeh ever think of gettin' out of here Georgie?

GEORGIE. To go where like?

EILEEN. I don't know. Anywhere. I mean let's face it Georgie, we might as well be livin' in the back of beyond as livin' here.

GEORGIE. How do you mean?

EILEEN. Style-wise. Music-wise. Sure by the time somethin' reaches us here it's already got out of date everywhere else.

GEORGIE. Aw I don't know about that now Eileen. I mean if a record comes out in England on a Monday say then you could nearly buy it downtown here the followin' weekend and that's not bad goin' for a little town like this.

EILEEN. Yeah well it's startin' to put years on me then. If it wasn't for me Daddy I'd be gone out of here long and ever ago . . .

SPEAKER. Newmarket weighed in. Weighed in at Newmarket.

EILEEN. Give us a shout if anyone is lookin' for me Georgie will yeh.

EILEEN *goes down to the office, a big ledger in her hand.* GEORGIE *watches her go.*

GEORGIE. Yeah right . . . She's a terrible nice girl Joe ain't she?

JOE. What?

GEORGIE. Eileen.

JOE. What about her?

GEORGIE. I say she's a fine girl.

JOE. Go away from me, will yeh. There's more mate on a butcher's apron. What did she mark down for third there?

GEORGIE. What? . . . The Loafer.

JOE. The Loafer. I thought so. I must remember that one. He should be worth a few bob the next time out. What price was he anyway?

GEORGIE (*sitting down on the bench, engrossed in a newspaper*). I don't know. Eight-to-one or somethin'. *Will Wexford regain the McCarty Cup?* Feckin' right we will. Jaysus look at the state of big Red O'Neill where he is. How would yeh like to be faced with the prospects of markin' that fella on Sunday now Joe? I'm goin' to tell yeh one thing but I don't think I'd sleep too well for the next couple of nights if it was me would you?

JOE. No.

GEORGIE. He's some big man though ain't he?

JOE. He is boy. There's no disputin' that alright.

STEVEN *enters from the office in his shirt sleeves.*

JOE. How's it goin' Steven?

STEVEN. Joe.

GEORGIE. Steven.

STEVEN. Georgie . . . Eileen where did yeh put that big ledger eh?

EILEEN (*off*). I have it Daddy. Why, are yeh wantin' it?

STEVEN. No, it's alright. I'll do it after.

JOE. Well Steven, I suppose you're travellin' up to the match on Sunday are yeh?

STEVEN. Yeah.

JOE. Can a duck swim, says you.

GEORGIE. How are yeh gettin' up to it, Steven?

STEVEN. I'm goin' up on that auld bus out of Larkin's pub.

GEORGIE. The same as ourselves. Jaysus it's a good deal though lads, ain't it? The bus, a meal and overnight accommodation for thirty-five quid. It's alright, ain't it?

JOE. We'll probably all end up sleepin' in the one bed. What do yeh think of our chances anyway, Steven?

STEVEN. Ah I don't know. When it gets to that level it could go either way.

JOE. That's a fact alright. There's a certain amount of luck involved in it all too ain't there?

STEVEN. Yeah – at that level, anyway.

JOE. Hey Steven, what do yeh think of all these women comin' along this year? Hah? I'm goin' to tell yeh one thing Steven, when you and me were runnin' the bus we had none of this auld codoligy did we? It was strictly a money on the counter, men only affair. These fellas haven't collected half the money nor nothin' yet I believe.

STEVEN. Will we get there at all?

JOE. Now you said it Steven. Will we get there at all is right. Hey Georgie did I hear you sayin' that some of the women below in the factory are comin'?

GEORGIE. Yeah. Big Mag Delaney and all.

JOE. Big Mag is comin' is she? Oh be Jaysus little Mickey Morris'll be away with it so.

GEORGIE. How's that?

JOE. Sure big Mag is dyin' alive about Mickey. She came down to our section the other day there Steven lookin' for Mickey to open this great tin of beans for her. She was back again that afternoon with another tin for him to open . . .

JOE *winks. The others look at each other.*

Two tins of beans in the one day Georgie. I mean what is she, a friggin' cowboy or somethin'. Jaysus man John Wayne wouldn't go through two tins of beans in the one day . . . Did yeh tell Steven about the jersey yeh got Georgie? Big Red O'Neill tossed his jersey out into the crowd after the Leinster Final and the queer fella here was the one that caught it.

GEORGIE. Aw yeh should have seen me Steven. I was like Lowry Mar goin' up to catch it boy. I'm goin' to tell yeh one thing lads but it'd take the three of us to fill it. You could nearly rear a family in it man.

JOE. Give it to big Mag Delaney. She'd be well able to fill it.

GEORGIE. Hey there's only one fella wearin' that jersey on Sunday and that's me. And I standin' that way for the Boys of Wexford.

GEORGIE *stands to rigid attention and then suddenly bursts into a commentator's voice.*

And it's a glorious day here today in Croke Park. The sun is absolutely splitting the trees and shining down on the hardy men from Cork and the sturdy Boys of Wexford. And the ball is in and the game is on and Tommy James has the ball and he sends a grand lobbing ball across to Big Red O'Neill who goes ploughing through the backs like a big rhinoceros. And he takes his shot and it's a long dropping ball and it's over the bar for a point for Wexford. Cuilín amháin le Loch Garman agus tá sé mahogany gaspipe. Tá sé bore the hole in the bucket . . . I'm goin' to tell yeh one thing lads but if Wexford don't win that match on Sunday I'll be fluthered drunk comin' home on that bus. And I'll be even worse if they do win.

STEVEN *smiles a sad smile and makes to leave, putting on his overcoat and scarf.*

STEVEN. Yeh might tell Eileen that I'm gone ahead home, Georgie will yeh.

GEORGIE. Yeah, right Steven.

STEVEN. Oh and tell her too not to bother about the evenin' paper. I'll get one meself.

GEORGIE. OK.

JOE. Good luck Steven.

STEVEN. All the best.

STEVEN *leaves*.

GEORGIE. Ole King Cole . . . Hey Joe yeh have to hand it to me though, I very nearly had him goin' that time didn't I? For a minute there I thought sure he was goin' to laugh, did you?

JOE. Huh, that'll be the day. Give us that paper there Georgie will yeh?

GEORGIE *brings it to him.*

GEORGIE. And did yeh see the big coat and scarf and all on him? I hope we don't get the weather he's expectin'. I wouldn't like to see him in the middle of the winter would you?

JOE. But sure that man is afraid of his life to let a bit of sun in at him Georgie.

MOLLY *enters from the back room with a bucket and mop in her hand.*

MOLLY. What won the last one Joe?

JOE. Elephant's Memory.

MOLLY *winces at the news.*

GEORGIE. Why, what did yeh back Molly?

MOLLY. Napper Tandy.

GEORGIE. He was well down the field Molly. Mind you he ran a good race for yeh though. The other horses had to gang up on him. It took about fourteen of them to bate him . . . You're just after missin' Ole King Cole. He told us a couple of right jokes and everything here, didn't he Joe?

MOLLY. I'd say that.

JOE. Oh that reminds me Molly, did you hear anything about Danger Doyle being back in town?

MOLLY. Who was tellin' yeh this?

JOE. Ah some auld one that was in here today was sayin' that she thought sure she saw Danger Doyle walkin' along the Main Street early this mornin' with a suitcase in his hand.

MOLLY. I never heard nothin' about it then . . .

JOE. Well the news is out that he's back.

Silence.

GEORGIE (*whistles at the news*). Danger Doyle!

MOLLY. I doubt it . . . Mind you I wouldn't put it past him.

JOE. That was always one thing about Danger boy. You could never put anything past him. I remember one day meself and him robbed the nun's orchard and Danger cut the arse off himself on a big piece of glass as we were gettin' out over the wall. The blood was pumpin' out of him I swear. And do you know what he done boy? He got down off the wall and – with his pockets bulgin' with apples now – he went around and knocked on the convent door to see if they'd be able to give him a plaster or somethin' to . . .

EILEEN *enters and a hush falls on the little congregation.*

GEORGIE. Hey Eileen, your Da was here lookin' for yeh. He's gone ahead home.

EILEEN. Oh thanks, Georgie.

GEORGIE. And he told me to tell yeh that he already got the evenin' paper.

JOE. He's gone home to study the form for the match on Sunday, Eileen. So you'd better keep your head down goin' in the door because they'll probably be hurlin' balls flyin' right, left and centre in there.

EILEEN. I'm well used to that Joe. (*She grabs a skewer of dockets and goes back down to the office.*)

GEORGIE. Would yeh say she heard us?

JOE. I don't know. Sure what harm if she did. If Danger is back in town she's goin' to have to get used to it anyway.

GEORGIE. Yeah, I suppose so.

MOLLY. Do yeh know somethin' boy, one of these days you're goin' to get a right hand for yourself so yeh are.

GEORGIE. What do yeh mean?

MOLLY. Yeh think the sun, moon and stars shines out of that one's face so yeh do. But like mother, like daughter is what I always say. Of course yeh won't be told.

MOLLY *goes down into the office.*

Silence. JOE *chuckles.*

GEORGIE. What?

JOE. Ah I'm just thinkin' about Danger. Jaysus he was some term boy I'm not coddin' yeh. 'Me Ma never even knew I drank,' says he, until I went home sober one day.' Poor auld Danger. We made fellas hop around here me and him I don't mind tellin' yeh. Me and Danger. We were the king pins in this town at the time so we were. Danger and me. Yes, the king pins we were . . . Did I ever tell yeh about all the times we used to break into this place?

GEORGIE. Yeah, yeh told me about that alright.

JOE. We used to break in through that big window there, the pair of us, and we'd stamp a docket for maybe five to three the next day or whenever and then when the race was over we'd just write in the winner of it and that was that. But of course the auld one that was workin' here at the time eventually twigged it and they set a trap for us. And do you want to know how she twigged it?

GEORGIE. The writin' was out in front of the stamp or somethin' wasn't it?

JOE. Yeah. The writin' was out in front of the stamp instead of it being the other way around yeh see. It should have been behind it. She got suspicious when we came in to collect on a fairly big bet that she couldn't remember us placin'. She started examinin' the docket then and that more or less gave the game away on us. Mind you we got away with it for a long time. We were queer and lucky not to be sent up the river that time boy.

MOLLY *traipses through the anteroom again.*

I'm just tellin' this fella here about all the queer things meself and Danger got up to Molly. Butch Cassidy and the Sundance Kid we were like weren't we?

MOLLY. Abbott and Costello would be more feckin' like it.

She goes into the back room.

JOE. She was dyin' alive about Danger.

GEORGIE (*surprised*). Who, Molly!

JOE. Yeah. Oh Molly was a fine hoult in her day boy.

Pause.

GEORGIE. I'd say you'd like to see him again alright would yeh?

JOE. Yeah. And not blowin' me own trumpet or anything but I think I can safely say that he wouldn't mind seein' me again either.

GEORGIE. He sounds like a right chancer goin' around.

JOE. Yeah he was. Oh now they didn't call him Danger Doyle for nothin' Georgie.

JOE *returns to the newspaper.* GEORGIE *loses himself in thought.* EILEEN *returns and begins working through the skewer of dockets again.*

EILEEN. Well Georgie, are yeh goin' up to the dance tonight or what?

GEORGIE. What? Oh definitely. Sure it wouldn't be the same without me Eileen would it?

EILEEN. No.

GEORGIE (*going to her*). Are yeh goin' up to it yourself?

EILEEN. Natch. What band is playin' tonight anyway?

GEORGIE. Lugs McGuire and the boys. Did yeh ever hear him playin' Joe?

JOE. Who's that?

GEORGIE. Lugs McGuire. He's great on the auld guitar boy. Lovely chords and all.

JOE. I heard that alright.

GEORGIE. Someone was tellin' me that he's after composin' a song about Red O'Neill to the tune of Yellow River. It's supposed to be brilliant I believe.

JOE. But sure how could he get out of it. His Ma was a great musician too. She used to play the accordion with The Toreadors. The only woman in town with purple nipples.

GEORGIE *laughs.*

EILEEN. Do you know somethin', you two are disgustin' so ye are . . .

JOE. What!

EILEEN *chuckles*.

EILEEN. Hey by the way Georgie, did yeh notice anythin' different about me today?

GEORGIE. No. What is it, your hair or somethin'?

EILEEN *displays a locket around her neck*.

EILEEN. Nice ain't it?

GEORGIE (*examining it*). Yeah, it's neat alright.

EILEEN. I've just stuck a picture of me Mammy in there for the time being. Later on I'll get a proper one of her mounted in it.

GEORGIE. What is it, gold or somethin'?

EILEEN. Yeah. I hope so anyway.

GEORGIE. Who's it from, your Ma?

EILEEN. Yeah. It just arrived this mornin' out of the blue.

GEORGIE. What is it, your birthday or somethin'?

EILEEN (*nods*). Tomorrow . . . It's a nice lookin' yoke though ain't it?

GEORGIE. Yeah. It's grand. Are yeh off Molly?

MOLLY *comes through the door, fastening her overcoat*.

MOLLY. Yeah.

GEORGIE. Are yeh goin' to come to the dance tonight?

MOLLY. I think my dancin' days are done boy.

GEORGIE. That's not what I heard then. Joe there was tellin' me that you were a right auld court in your heyday.

MOLLY. What the hell would he know about it? That fella'd shit himself now if he got a good court. I'll see yeh in the mornin' Eileen.

EILEEN. Yeah, see yeh Molly.

MOLLY *leaves*.

JOE. Thanks very much Georgie.

GEORGIE. She's some nettle ain't she?

JOE. She is boy! She's the contrariest woman I ever met and that's sayin' somethin' because I'm married to a one who can turn the milk sour with a glance first thing in the mornin', but I'm goin' to tell yeh one thing she's not a patch on her.

EILEEN. Oh I don't think I'd like to cross Molly somehow or other.

JOE. No, nor I either Eileen.

JOE *rises and goes out to the toilet. Pause.*

EILEEN. Hey Georgie, do yeh still hang around Byrne's Café these days?

GEORGIE. Yeah sometimes. How come I don't see you around there this weather?

EILEEN. But sure I only went in there when I was goin' out with Johnny Doran like yeh know.

GEORGIE. Oh that's right, Doraney was one of the king pins down there alright – on the machines and all. Well he thought he was anyway.

EILEEN *smiles fondly at* GEORGIE.

EILEEN. Is, 'One Way Love' still on the jukebox down there?

GEORGIE. Yeah Number 4B.

EILEEN. Aw is it? I love that do you?

GEORGIE. Yeah it's alright. Lugs McGuire and the boys plays that yeh know?

EILEEN. Do they?

GEORGIE. Yeah.

He sings.

> Must I always sing the same old song
> Every time I turn around you're gone
> Won't somebody tell me where do I belong . . .

EILEEN *singing softly while she works.*

> While you're up there and I'm sinkin' fast
> You must be livin' in a plastercast
> I don't want to spend my nights just thinkin' of
> One way love.

GEORGIE *stands there, drinking in the very sight of her and the lilt of her voice.*

EILEEN. There's only one thing I can't figure out about all of this though Georgie. The locket I mean . . . Accordin' to the guarantee it was bought down town in Carrington's.

GEORGIE. What's wrong with that?

EILEEN. Yeah but I mean what did she do, ring up Carrington's from London or what?

GEORGIE. Yeah, she probably did.

EILEEN. But sure she could have posted somethin' like this no bother. Anyway the card was written in her own handwritin' . . . I'm just wonderin' now if maybe me Mammy's in town, that maybe she came home for a bit of a holiday or somethin'.

GEORGIE. Naw. You would have heard somethin' Eileen.

EILEEN *sighs and touches the locket.*

EILEEN. I'm dyin' to see her again though Georgie. I know I'm always goin' on about her and all but . . . Ah I don't know. Ten years is a long time and a picture in a locket is not the same as the real thing, is it? It'll be her anniversary on Monday, yeh know?

GEORGIE. What do yeh mean?

EILEEN. It was the day after the All Ireland Final that she went away, sure. Yeh know I haven't got a clue what Danger Doyle looks like but I keep imaginin' that he's real handsome – like someone you'd see in the pictures. Jack Nicholson or someone.

GEORGIE. Jack Nicholson! He's not good lookin'.

EILEEN. Ah he is Georgie. I think he is anyway. I think he's deadly lookin'. Why who would you call good lookin' now?

GEORGIE. I don't know. Big Red O'Neill or someone.

EILEEN. Ah go away out of that Georgie, a big farmer goin' around.

GEORGIE. I'm tellin' yeh Eileen, come Sunday every woman in the town'll be after him because he's the man who's goin' to take us there. That's who you should be puttin' in your locket, girl . . . Hey Joe, show Eileen that picture in the paper of Big Red.

JOE (*returning*). What?

GEORGIE. I say I'm just tellin' Eileen here that Big Red is the man who's goin' to take us there on Sunday.

JOE. He'd better Georgie because I'm goin' to put a fiver on them now. If he don't score three or four goals this Sunday his photograph is comin' down off of my mantelpiece and that's all's about it.

GEORGIE. That's what I like about Joe. He's patriotic to the core.

JOE. When there's money at stake, Georgie, my allegiance goes out the window. Are yeh wantin' to come in on it with me? (JOE *is writing out a docket.*)

GEORGIE. What? Yeah, alright . . . Hey Eileen I'll get yeh that record for your birthday – 'One Way Love', I mean.

EILEEN. No yeh won't. You can't afford to be spendin' money on me at all. It's alright Georgie, I'll get it meself durin' the week.

GEORGIE. No I'll get it for yeh. Anyway who said anythin' about spendin' money. By this time tomorrow number 4B will be gone missin' from Byrne's jukebox.

JOE (*handing GEORGIE a docket and money*). Here boy, go make yourself useful.

EILEEN. Georgie Whelan, don't you dare do that. I don't want you gettin' in any trouble over me at all. Anyway the centre is always gone out of those jukebox records. Georgie do yeh hear me talkin' to yeh.

GEORGIE. Stop fussin' woman will yeh.

JOE. Come on Georgie will yeh, 'til I go and get the tay.

GEORGIE, *a broad grin on his face, hands* EILEEN *the docket.*

EILEEN (*stamping the docket*). You're not to, Georgie.

GEORGIE *chuckles and examines the money in his hand.*

GEORGIE. Hey Joe, what's goin' on here?

JOE (*buttoning his coat up*). What? Yeah! You owe me a pound from the other day.

JOE *takes the docket and leaves.*

Lights down.

Scene Two

Lights up on the betting shop. EILEEN *is behind the counter.* MOLLY *is singing 'Dream Lover', as she works, dusting and polishing etc.*

MOLLY. Well Eileen, was the dance any use last night after?

EILEEN. Yeah it was alright. I enjoyed it anyway.

MOLLY. Yeh don't sound too enthusiastic about it then? The talent must have been scarce on the ground or somethin' was it?

EILEEN. Ah the usual yeh know. Sure all the nice fellas are gone Molly.

MOLLY. Hey Eileen, forget about the nice fellas. It's the bold boys yeh'd want to get your hands on. They're more fun. It's someone with a bit of jiss in him yeh'd want. Anyway what's all this sudden interest in nice fellas? I thought you were supposed to be partial to the wild boys.

EILEEN. What do yeh mean?

MOLLY. But sure weren't you all great with your man who ran away with the carnival last year. Whatshisname . . . Johnny Doran?

EILEEN. Oh yeah. Johnny was a bit wild alright.

MOLLY. A bit wild is puttin' it mildly I think Eileen. Didn't someone have a baby for him recently there?

EILEEN. Yeah.

MOLLY. That's not his picture you've got in that locket that you keep playin' with is it?

EILEEN. No. That's me Mammy.

MOLLY. Mmn . . . I'd say you were fairly fond of him though Eileen were yeh?

EILEEN *shrugs.*

What?

EILEEN. I don't know. He was different yeh know. He was a right bit of laugh and he was . . . Ah I don't know. He was just sort of different, that's all.

MOLLY. I know what yeh mean hon. I used to know a fella like that one time meself. Jaysus he's was a real hardcase too goin' around – swaggerin' about the place, puttin' on the agony as they say.

EILEEN. What happened to him?

MOLLY. What . . .? He went away . . . So this was a present from your Ma was it?

MOLLY *touches the locket.*

EILEEN. Yeah.

MOLLY. Yeh must have a roomful of stuff from her by now have yeh?

EILEEN. I surely have. You can hardly get into my bedroom with all the things me Mammy is after sendin' me over the years – toys and books and dolls and all. And as for jewellery! I've a music box that's absolutely overflowin' with jewellery. I mean I literally can't fit anythin' else into it.

MOLLY. Yeah well my advice to you is to take all yeh can get from her while it's goin' because it's not goin' to last yeh know.

EILEEN. What do yeh mean?

MOLLY. If I know your Ma as soon as you begin to blossom she won't want to know yeh. She don't like anyone tryin' to muscle in on her territory yeh see . . . I remember her down in Byrne's Café years ago and she swishin' across to the jukebox, a great skin-tight jeans on her and all. I'll give her one thing, when she walked across a room heads turned. She was a little older than me and I remember thinkin' at the time that as soon as she moved on I'd take her place.

EILEEN. And did yeh?

MOLLY. She never moved on. She hung back to claim the heart of the latest little tearaway in town. She did that for years.

EILEEN. What about me Daddy?

MOLLY. She met him at a dance somewhere. None of us could believe it when it was announced that they were gettin' married. A few weeks before she was ridin' around on the back of somebody else's motor bike. If she was here today she'd probably be dancin' cheek to cheek with Johnny Doran or someone. Huh, speakin' of wild fellas.

GEORGIE *has just entered, dressed up in his good suit and carrying an overnight bag.*

Well Georgie, any joy at the dance last night?

GEORGIE. Naw.

MOLLY. Ah go away out of that boy, you're a dead loss so yeh are. Eileen is only after tellin' me that there was lashin's of talent there last night.

GEORGIE. Yeah well I didn't see a whole lot of it then.

EILEEN. Thanks very much Georgie.

GEORGIE. What?

MOLLY. Get out of it Georgie Whelan, yeh wouldn't get off in Hyde Park with a fiver in your hand.

GEORGIE. I'm goin' to tell yeh one thing but some of them there last night would nearly want to pay me a fiver just to dance with them.

MOLLY. God blast yeh anyway, anyone'd think he was Robert Redford or someone goin' around. Hey I like the suit Eileen, do you? Ain't he all out in his coughdrops now? Me Da got married in a suit just like that yeh know?

GEORGIE. Did he? Were yeh at the weddin' yourself?

MOLLY. Get out of it yeh little get yeh before I break your feckin' face for yeh.

GEORGIE *laughs.*

EILEEN. It won't be long now, Georgie.

GEORGIE. No. The bus should be pullin' in any minute now and then we'll hit the high road.

MOLLY. Have yeh no fancy hat to wear?

GEORGIE. I don't need a fancy hat Molly. I have this. (*He pulls out a massive jersey from his bag and holds it up to the light.*)

EILEEN. Where did yeh get that Georgie?

GEORGIE. Believe it or not this once belonged to the great Red O'Neill. He whipped it off of him after the Leinster Final and he tossed it out into the crowd and yours truly was the one who caught it.

MOLLY. By Jaysus you'll be a fine fella when that fits yeh.

GEORGIE. I will won't I? The size of it! I'll be wearin' this jersey tomorrow at the match. What am I talkin' about, I'll probably be wearin' this in the bed in that hotel tonight. That's provided that I get to bed at all of course.

STEVEN *enters*.

Well Steven, what do yeh think of that then?

STEVEN. What?

GEORGIE. This is the jersey I was tellin' yeh about. Red O'Neill's. I'll be a fine fella when that fits me won't I?

STEVEN. Yeah . . . (*He goes down to the office.*) Eileen, where did yeh put that big flask eh?

EILEEN. I don't know Daddy. Is it not on top of the cabinet there?

STEVEN (*off*). What?

EILEEN. Or in the big drawer maybe.

STEVEN. It's alright, I found it.

MOLLY. What do yeh think of the locket she got Steven? It's a nice lookin' yoke ain't it?

STEVEN. Yeah.

MOLLY. Ain't it well for her? So are yeh all set for tomorrow Steven?

EILEEN *fills the flask with tea*.

STEVEN. Yeah. All set. Just waitin' on the auld bus to arrive now and we'll be off.

GEORGIE (*putting the jersey away*). Any sign of it yet Steven?

STEVEN. No. No sign of it yet.

MOLLY. Are we goin' to win Steven?

STEVEN. I don't know that. To tell yeh the truth so long as it's a good, hard and clean game I'm not that pushed which way it goes.

MOLLY. Mmn . . . I'd prefer to win it meself. You can keep your hard and clean game so long as we win it. Maybe that sounds a bit primitive but . . .

STEVEN. Ah no. Everyone has their own way of lookin' at it. So long as you row in behind your team that's all that counts.

MOLLY. Is it?

STEVEN. Yeah. Get behind your team. Get behind your town.

MOLLY. Do you hear that Georgie? You're to get behind your town. I bet yeh Steven has a fancy hat to wear tomorrow have yeh Steven?

STEVEN. What?

MOLLY. I say I bet you have a fancy hat to . . . Ah don't tell me you have n'er a hat either. Jaysus what kind of fellas are ye at all eh?

STEVEN *goes across and lays a little parcel of money on the counter for* EILEEN – *some silver wrapped up in a few pound notes.*

STEVEN. There's a few bob for your birthday hon.

EILEEN. Oh thanks very much Daddy.

STEVEN *smiles.*

MOLLY. He didn't forget yeh, all the same Eileen. Hey Steven, what's all this I hear about a crowd of women goin' along to the match this year? I hope there'll be no hanky-panky goin' on up there now?

STEVEN. I'll see yeh tomorrow night, Eileen.

EILEEN. Right Daddy. Enjoy yourself.

MOLLY. Don't do anythin' I wouldn't do now Steven.

STEVEN *ill at ease, leaves.* EILEEN *and* MOLLY *look at each other.* MOLLY *goes out into the back room.*

GEORGIE (*oblivious to the whole thing*). Oh that reminds me Eileen, I have somethin' for you too. (*He takes the record from his bag and hands it to her.*)

EILEEN. What? I don't believe it. 'One Way Love'. Jesus. Thanks Georgie. I'm goin' to tell yeh one thing but I dearly hope that the cops won't be after me for this.

GEORGIE. No you'll be alright Eileen. I was wearin' kid gloves at the time. The centre is gone out of it but that's no bother to fix. I'm nearly certain I have a centre piece at home anyway. It just sort of clips into it like, yeh know. It's alright though ain't it?

EILEEN. It's grand. I'll play this to death all day tomorrow now.

GEORGIE. Yeah I know. You'll probably drive half the street demented. It serves 'em right anyway for not goin' up to the match.

EILEEN. 4B missin' from Byrne's jukebox.

GEORGIE. What? Yeah. There'll be big headlines in next week's paper. 4B missin' from Byrne's jukebox. A special version of 'One Way Love' which was imported direct from the UK.

EILEEN. Ah no Georgie, me heart wouldn't be able for it.

GEORGIE. I'm goin' to tell yeh one thing if they call to my house I'll say . . . (*He gives a little whistle and points to her.*)

EILEEN. I'll tell them you gave it to me.

GEORGIE. I'll deny all knowledge. I'll say fingerprint me. Don't worry about it Eileen, I'll come and visit yeh when you're inside, bring yeh banana sandwiches and all.

EILEEN *laughs, her whole face radiating. She reaches out and kisses* GEORGIE *on the cheek.*

EILEEN. Thanks very much Georgie. I'd better put it away before somebody sees it.

She puts the record under the counter. GEORGIE *watches her, spellbound.* JOE *enters.*

JOE. Do yeh know what boy but I'm queer and glad that I've nothin' to do with the organisin' of that big bus.

EILEEN. Why, what happened Joe?

JOE. Little Mickey Morris is fast asleep on the counter already and two other lads are threatenin' to box over who's goin' to sit in the front seat.

JOE *waves it all away.* MOLLY *enters.*

MOLLY. Look at him all done up to go to a feckin' auld match.

JOE. The All Ireland Final Molly.

MOLLY. Huh.

GEORGIE. Who are you goin' to be cheerin' for tomorrow Molly?

MOLLY. None of 'em. I hope the two of them lose. A waste of bloody money so it is. And I'm only after washin' that floor so none of you need go traipsin' across it at all.

MOLLY *goes into the office.*

JOE. I heard that song that young Lugs McGuire made up about Red O'Neill after.

GEORGIE. Did yeh? Why is he over in Larkin's?

JOE. Yeah, he's over there with the auld guitar and all. Jaysus it's good ain't it?

GEORGIE. Aw it's very well put together alright. The boys played it last night at the dance.

JOE (*sings*).
   Who's the one who can take us there
   To Croke Park or anywhere
   Who's the man that they all fear
   Red O'Neill is
   Red O'Neill is

GEORGIE *joins in.*

   Red O'Neill is
   Red O'Neill is
   Da da da da da da
   Red O'Neill is
   Red O'Neill is
   Da da da da da da . . .

They run out of words.

JOE. I'm goin' to tell yeh one thing boy but that could be a hit – in this country anyway.

Pause.

GEORGIE. Where's your bag Joe?

JOE. It's over in Larkin's pub.

GEORGIE. Have yeh much stuff?

JOE. No.

Silence.

EILEEN. Hey Georgie, did you hear anythin' about Danger Doyle being back in town?

GEORGIE. What? Oh yeah, I heard somethin' about that alright.

EILEEN. So it looks like I was wrong about me Mammy comin' home then?

GEORGIE. Yeah . . . it looks like it.

Pause.

EILEEN. And have yeh any idea where he's stayin'?

GEORGIE. No. Do you know where he's stayin' Joe?

JOE. I heard he was stoppin' down in the County Hotel.

EILEEN *nods and nervously touching her locket she bends her head to her work.*

Lights down.

Scene Three

Lights up on the betting shop. GEORGIE *is sitting in the alcove of the bay window while* JOE *paces up and down the floor irritably.*

JOE. Lord Jaysus ain't this awful, ain't it? We should have left this street three quarters of an hour ago nearly. I don't know . . . This is ridiculous now so it is.

EILEEN *comes out from behind the partition.*

Well Eileen, what did he say?

EILEEN. He said the bus left the garage about twenty minutes ago.

JOE. Twenty minutes ago! By Jaysus he must be comin' via the friggin' Alps then. Did yeh tell him I was on the verge of losin' the head here?

EILEEN. Yeah, I told him that.

JOE. What did he say?

EILEEN. He said, 'So what else is new?'

JOE (*amused*). Did he? (*He chuckles.*) . . . Well i'll give them about another five or ten minutes and then the deal is off.

EILEEN. Georgie keep an eye on the place for me there will yeh? I'm just wantin' to see me Daddy for a minute.

GEORGIE (*in a trance*). Yeah right.

JOE. Don't be too long Eileen because we're goin' the minute that bus arrives.

EILEEN. I won't be long. Sure I'll see the bus from the pub anyway. (*She goes.*)

JOE. I don't know. I'm not coddin' yeh boy they wouldn't be able to run a whorehouse, most of them. Yes, they wouldn't run a whorehouse.

GEORGIE (*out of the blue*). It must be great to have your own girl Joe, is it?

JOE. What?

GEORGIE. Yeh know someone to dance with and all. Someone to take home. Maybe bring her to the pictures now and again.

JOE. But sure there's lashin's of girls out there to dance with.

GEORGIE. Yeah I know but it's not the same as havin' your own girl though is it? I'd like to have me own girl now.

JOE. Is that what you were thinkin' about all this time?

GEORGIE. What?

JOE. I was wonderin' why you were so quiet.

GEORGIE. I wasn't quiet.

MOLLY *enters.*

JOE. You were like a little mouse there so yeh were.

MOLLY. What's wrong with him now?

JOE. Oh he's thinkin' about Eileen again.

GEORGIE. I never even mentioned Eileen.

MOLLY. Do yeh know somethin' boy, he absolutely worships the ground that that one walks on, don't he? But you'll get a right kick in the arse one of these days boy when yeh wake up to find that she's not all that she's made out to be.

GEORGIE. Will you go away out of that Molly, nobody's all they're made out to be accordin' to you.

MOLLY. Yeah and her even more so . . . You can laugh all yeh like boy but you'll rue the day that yeh ever laid eyes on that one yet, so yeh will, you mark my words.

MOLLY *picks up the mop and bucket and goes down into the back room.*

GEORGIE. All I said was that I wouldn't mind havin' me own girl.

JOE. You're lookin' for someone special though Georgie.

GEORGIE. And what's wrong with that? Look I just want to make sure that I don't end up with someone who's goin' to turn into Molly the minute I turn me back on her.

JOE. They're all in danger of turnin' into Molly son. The same as you're in danger of turnin' into me.

GEORGIE. What?

JOE. Yeah. Strange as it may seem I was once just like you yeh know – a little Jack the Shillin' goin' around who didn't know his arse from his elbow. And look at me now! It's all before yeh boy . . . It's all before yeh.

Pause.

GEORGIE. Don't mind me askin' yeh Joe, but what's Molly always hintin' at about Eileen?

JOE. What do yeh mean?

GEORGIE. Every time she catches me lookin' at Eileen or talkin' about her she tries to make out that there's somethin' goin' on that I don't know about.

JOE. Ah yeh know Molly. She's probably tryin' to make out that Eileen is the same as her Ma at the back of it – a bit of a skeet goin' around.

GEORGIE. How can she say that Joe?

JOE. Well there was a bit of a rumour goin' around last year alright that when Eileen was goin' out with your man who ran away with the circus or the carnival or whatever . . .

GEORGIE. Johnny Doran?

JOE. Yeah, young Doran.

GEORGIE. What about him?

JOE. Ah there was a bit of a rumour goin' around that he managed to get Eileen into the bed one time while Ole King Cole was away at a match somewhere.

GEORGIE. Who told yeh that?

JOE. No one in particular told me Georgie. It was just a rumour.

GEORGIE. I never heard nothin' about it then.

JOE. Yeah well I suppose nobody had the heart to tell yeh seein' how yeh practically genuflect every time Eileen's name is mentioned . . . Anyway it was just a rumour.

GEORGIE *is devastated.* JOE *continues to pace up and down.*

Aw this is disgraceful. Look at the time it is. Well I'm goin' to give them about five more minutes and then I'm goin' over to Larkin's to demand me money back. If they can't keep up their end of the bargain then I don't see why I should be expected to keep mine . . .

DANGER DOYLE *is standing in the doorway.*

DANGER. Are you still givin' out boy?

JOE. What? Who's that? Danger Doyle, me auld segotia, what way are yeh at all? Come in . . .

DANGER. Come in, he says. Anyone'd think that he owned the place or somethin'.

JOE. I'm goin' to tell yeh one thing Danger but I must have a share in it at this stage. Put it there me auld stock, long time no see.

They shake hands.

DANGER. How are yeh keepin' Joe?

JOE. Alright. Jaysus Danger, it's a queer long time since I saw you last boy.

DANGER. It's a long time alright Joe – nine, nearly ten years now sure.

JOE. What? Yeah it would be . . . I don't mind tellin' yeh but yeh caused a fair bit of a stir around here too yeh fucker yeh.

DANGER. What before I left yeh mean?

JOE. Before and after. For a long time after.

DANGER. Yeah, I can imagine. I suppose I was the talk of the town was I?

JOE. Danger, your name echoed from every dance hall in the land boy . . . So how is herself?

DANGER. Grand. Right form.

JOE. She didn't come over with yeh, no?

DANGER. No.

JOE. Ah sure, that's the way! So what did yeh do, come home to see the auld match or what?

DANGER. What? Oh yeah. I came back to see the auld match. . . . Who's that?

MOLLY *is singing, 'Stranger in Paradise'.*

JOE. What? That's your auld flame Danger . . . Molly! Someone must have told her she had legs like a lark . . . Hey what do yeh think of this lad, Danger? Matty Whelan's son. That's Danger Doyle now boy and yeh dyin' to meet him.

DANGER. But sure he wouldn't remember me. He'd have only been a nipper when I went away.

JOE. He heard of yeh though, Danger. Hey Georgie, show him the jersey yeh got. He got a jersey a few weeks ago off of big Red O'Neill. Where is it Georgie?

GEORGIE. It's in the bag there.

JOE *takes the jersey out of the bag and holds it up.*

JOE. What do yeh make of that Danger? Feel the heft of it. You'd want to be Charles Atlas to lift it nearly. He'll be a fine fella when that fits him won't he? Of course these fellas think they're big lads goin' around here yeh know? They think they're the bees knees so they do. I mean I try to tell them the way it used to be with you and me but sure . . . We made fellas hop around here, me and him. Didn't we Danger? I was just tellin' Georgie the other day about all the times we used to break into this place and how they'd never have caught us at all if it hadn't 've been for the auld one who spotted that the writin' was out in front of the stamp. Jaysus we made some money out of it boy. How many times did we knock off this place Danger before they copped on?

DANGER. Twice.

JOE. What? Ah no it was more than that Danger.

DANGER. We broke in here twice. We made thirty bob each on the first transaction and they had a trap set for us the second time round. I climbed in through that big bay window there. You were outside keepin' nix. Or supposed to be keepin' nix I should say.

JOE. That's right, I had hurt me foot or somethin' hadn't I?

DANGER. Yeah. Anyway, the next thing I know I've set off some
sort of an alarm and there was cops swarmin' all over me. No
sign of your man here at all of course.

JOE. I whistled out to yeh Danger.

DANGER. Yes yeh did yeah. Yeh must have whistled under your
breath then because I never heard yeh. I wouldn't mind but yeh
could hear a pin drop in the place the same night. Suddenly
anyway there's cops comin' in through every door and window in
the shop and that big cop whatshisname is tryin' to grab a hold
of me. Sanders.

JOE. Oh yeah, Big Sanders. He was a right bastard that fella was
wasn't he?

DANGER. I took a swing at him and he downed me with a box in
the jaw. I wasn't much of a hard case after that. Me knees just
buckled from in under me I swear. Then he picked me up and
shagged me into the back of the squad car like an auld sack of
potatoes.

JOE. We all went up to the courtroom the next day, a whole crowd
of us – do yeh remember Danger? I'll never forget that boy.
Poor Danger gettin' led in with a great pair of handcuffs on him
and he nearly cryin'. It was queer funny.

DANGER. What do yeh mean nearly cryin? I was cryin'. I'm goin'
to tell yeh one thing but it's a good job I wasn't able to get at you
that time because I'd 've kilt yeh.

JOE. I whistled out to yeh Danger.

DANGER *sighs, turns away chuckling*.

DANGER (*turning to* GEORGIE *with the jersey*). So when did he give
yeh this then?

GEORGIE. After the Leinster final. He just tossed it out into the
crowd and I caught it.

DANGER. He's a good hurler ain't he?

GEORGIE. Yeah.

JOE. He's the best, Danger . . . So what does it feel like to be
home, boy?

DANGER. What do it feel like? . . . I'll tell yeh lads, today I found
meself snakin' through the streets of me own hometown like a
whatdoyoucallit . . . Ah I can't think of the word now.

JOE. A fugitive, Danger. Like a fugitive.

DANGER. Yeah. A fugitive.

MOLLY *enters.*

MOLLY. Are youse not gone yet? It'll be nearly time to come back before yeh leave at all.

JOE. What do yeh think of this fella Molly?

MOLLY. Who's that?

DANGER. How are yeh, honey bunch?

MOLLY. How are yeh? When did you get home?

DANGER. Yesterday mornin'.

MOLLY. Had yeh a good crossin'?

DANGER. Yeah it was alright. A bit bumpy at times like, yeh know but . . . it was alright.

MOLLY. I heard you were back alright but to tell you the truth I was hard set to believe it.

DANGER. Why's that?

JOE. Good man, Danger.

MOLLY. So how long are yeh stayin' for anyway?

DANGER. I don't know. A couple of days.

JOE. He came over to see the auld match, Molly. Hey Georgie, keep an eye out for that bus there will yeh?

JOE *goes out to the toilet.*

DANGER. So how are yeh keepin' anyway, Molly?

MOLLY. How do I look?

DANGER. You look grand.

MOLLY. Do I?

DANGER. Yeah . . . Were yeh surprised to see me?

MOLLY. Yeah I was. But then you were always full of surprises weren't yeh?

DANGER. Was I?

MOLLY. Give us a fag will yeh?

He gives her a cigarette and lights her up.

Jaysus look at me. I'm shakin' like a leaf here.

DANGER. Why?

MOLLY. Because I've just seen a ghost that's why.

DANGER. Is that what I am, a ghost?

MOLLY. Yeah, for want of a better word.

DANGER. Yeah well, don't worry about it hon. I didn't come back here to haunt you.

MOLLY. You didn't need to come back to do that Danger.

JOE (*returning*). Anythin' stirrin' Georgie?

GEORGIE. No.

JOE. Hah? Lord Jaysus ain't this awful ain't it!

He storms towards the front door.

I'll see yeh tomorrow night in Larkin's, Danger, as soon as we get back. That's if we ever get there in the first place of course. Where are yeh stoppin' anyway?

DANGER. The County Hotel.

JOE. Huh, swanky. I'll see yeh, Danger.

DANGER. Good luck Joe . . . He seems to be in right form anyway. I was often readin' about him in the local paper. He's into everythin' ain't he? Darts and football and what have yeh. Jaysus every time yeh turn a page there he is starin' up at yeh.

MOLLY. Yeah well Joe woke up one mornin' to find that there was a great big hole in his life yeh see. He's been tryin' to fill it up ever since . . . But sure I'll probably see yeh meself in Larkin's tomorrow night. I'll let yeh buy me a drink – for old time's sake.

She leaves. Silence.

DANGER. How is your Da, Georgie?

GEORGIE. Well, thanks. Sure, why don't yeh go on up to the house and see him?

DANGER. Ah no, I don't think so.

GEORGIE. Why not? I'd say he'd be delighted to see yeh.

Pause.

DANGER. Hey Georgie, have yeh any idea where Eileen is?

GEORGIE. She just slipped across to the pub for a minute to see her Da.

DANGER. Would yeh be able to go over and get her for me?

GEORGIE. But sure she'll be back in a minute.

DANGER. Yeah I know but I really don't want to hang around here too long like, yeh know.

GEORGIE *thinks about it. He acquiesces.*

DANGER. Good man Georgie. She's not goin' up to the match or anythin' is she?

GEORGIE. No.

JOE (*from the doorway*). Come on Georgie, we're bailin' out . . . The bus is here.

GEORGIE. Oh yeah, right. Any sign of Eileen?

JOE. She's on her way, come on. I told her you were here, Danger.

DANGER. Thanks Joe.

JOE. Come on Georgie, will yeh. There y'are now Danger, you'll have the run of the place to yourself. That's a right turn for the books alright ain't it? Come on Georgie.

JOE *leaves.*

GEORGIE (*stuffing the jersey back into his bag*). So how long are yeh goin' to hang around for anyway?

DANGER. I'm goin' back tomorrow evenin', Georgie, and I'm goin' to tell yeh one thing but it'll be a queer long time before you see me again boy . . . You'll be well after fillin' out that jersey by then so yeh will.

GEORGIE. We'll have a long wait for that I think.

DANGER. But sure what harm if yeh never fill it out Georgie. Aren't yeh big enough?

GEORGIE *exits.* DANGER *rambles around the shop, taking in his surroundings.* EILEEN *enters.*

How are yeh Eileen?

EILEEN. Hello.

DANGER. Do yeh know somethin', the smell out of this auld place brings back a queer lot of memories for me, I can tell yeh.

EILEEN. Does it? I didn't realise it had a smell of its own. What does it smell of anyway?

DANGER. Misfortune . . . How are yeh doin'?

EILEEN. Alright. Was that you who got me the locket from Carrington's, yeah?

DANGER. Yeah. Ah your Mammy asked me to get yeh somethin' for your birthday. I just thought I might as well get it over here, save me luggin' it all the way across. Was it alright for yeh after?

EILEEN. Yeah it was lovely. Thanks. Is me Mammy OK?

DANGER. Yeah. She's alright. She misses you terrible of course. She was wonderin' if maybe you'd come back with me – spend a bit of time with her.

EILEEN. Go back to London with yeh, yeh mean?

DANGER. Yeah. Just for a little while. Stay until Christmas maybe. What do yeh think?

EILEEN. I don't know.

DANGER. Well I mean to say you're not exactly over the moon about workin' here are yeh? Not accordin' to your letters anyway.

EILEEN. No, I'm not mad about the job but . . .

DANGER. Well there y'are then.

EILEEN. Is there no chance of me Mammy comin' over here?

DANGER. Naw, I don't think so, Eileen.

EILEEN *thinks about it and sighs*.

EILEEN. It's just that me Daddy might think that I was . . .

DANGER. What? Look if you're wantin' me to talk to him, just say so. I mean to say, Eileen, it's only for a couple of months.

Pause.

EILEEN. When are yeh goin' back anyway?

DANGER. Tomorrow evenin' . . . I have to be back at work be Monday night yeh see.

EILEEN (*angrily*). I just don't see why she can't come over here.

SPEAKER. Runners and riders at Kelso as in your morning
papers. Non-runners at Newmarket, Number Seven, The Baker's
Wife and Number Nine, Italian Lady. Number Seven and
Number Nine, non-runners at Newmarket.

EILEEN *goes behind the counter to mark off the non-runners on the
result sheet. Then she comes out to repeat the process on the sheet above
the bench.* DANGER *watches her.*

DANGER. Your Ma don't like the idea of you workin' here at all,
yeh know.

EILEEN (*sulkily*). Why's that?

DANGER. Ah, I don't know. I think she keeps imaginin' all the
hard cases and chancers that are comin' in and out of here all
the time.

EILEEN. Most of them are alright.

Pause as EILEEN *fiddles with the locket.*

DANGER. Your Mammy'd love to come back here Eileen – to see
you, to see your little room and all. But let's face it, it's not as
simple as that is it? Jaysus hon, around here they'd turn the poor
crator to dust so they would . . . (*Pause.*) Yeh know I can still
remember one of the very first presents your Mammy ever
bought for you. It was a little sort of a music box. When yeh
opened the lid a tune spilled out of it. We bought it in a shop in
Shepherds Bush market. Heidelmann or somethin' was your
man's name who owned the shop. He stamped his name on the
cardboard box it came in. Jewish I think he was. 'Eileen'd love
that now' your Mammy said when she saw it in the window, a
great fancy design on it and all. Jaysus there was more wrappin'
went on that present than little . . . What's up Eileen?

EILEEN *is weeping.*

EILEEN. I don't know. It's all so sudden. One minute I'm here,
the next you want to just whisk me away. I'm not like you, yeh
know. I can't just do things on the spur of the moment. I've me
Daddy to think of.

DANGER. Yeah well I must confess I always was a spur of the
moment man alright. Did yeh know I once climbed up to the top
of Rowe Street chapel and hung me hat on the steeple. I just saw
the ladders there, took a figeary and up I went. And another
time we were all at this dance in the Town Hall and the County
Manager's daughter was at it. I'm not coddin' yeh, nobody had

the nerve to ask the girl up for a dance. So I just went over and asked her. She got up with me too . . . Your Mammy's terrible depressed, yeh know. She's on these auld tablets and all. I think if she saw you again she might be alright. Yeh should have come over to see her by now anyway Eileen . . .! She never stops talkin' about you, yeh know. I'm not coddin' yeh, she never stops. Eileen! Eileen! Eileen! – mornin', noon, and night.

Pause as EILEEN *looks into his sad eyes.*

EILEEN. Me Daddy 'll go mad . . .

EILEEN *goes and sits in the alcove of the bay window. Silence.*

DANGER (*moving closer to her*). Reinmann was his name though not Heidelmann. Reinmann – the fella that sold us the music box. He had a scutty shop in Shepherds Bush market. Bracelets and rings and that kind of thing. It had a galvanised roof. When it rained you could hardly hear your ears in the place. Some auld fella had slipped on a little rainbow of oil in the street that day. I picked him up and brought him into the shop, put him sittin' down on a chair. Your man made him a cup of tea. He was a nice enough fella – Reinmann. Stamped his name on nearly everythin' he sold. We were drenched that day goin' around in the rain, your Mammy and me. I had a great big hole in me shoe I remember, and your Mammy had one of those enormous headscarves wrapped around her. She looked really pale. I got a bit of a fright when I caught a glimpse of her in a shop window – her pale face hidin' behind the rain. When we got back to the auld flat we were livin' in, I lit a fire and she sat hunched over it for hours on end starin' into the flames with the music box on her lap. I think that's when it began to dawn on me that there was a certain corner of her heart that I'd never be able to sweep clean.

Silence. DANGER *looks down to see* EILEEN *staring up at him, tears in her eyes.*

Do yeh fancy havin' your tea with me this evenin' down in the County Hotel?

EILEEN (*tearfully*). That'd be nice.

DANGER. A high tea on a low table hah?

EILEEN *looks into his eyes and smiles sadly.* DANGER *slowly rises and leaves.*

SPEAKER. The one fifteen at Newmarket. Royal York three-to-one. Splash seven-to-two. Time Out and The Tablemaker six-to-one. Tar and Feathered thirteen-to-two Daffy's Lad eight-to-one. Cool as a Breeze and Haymaker . . .

EILEEN *rises. She goes to the result sheet to mark up the horses. She breaks down and cries.*

Lights down.

ACT TWO

Scene One

The betting shop. EILEEN *is behind the counter working her way through a skewer of dockets. There is a suitcase standing close by.* MOLLY *enters.*

MOLLY. What's up Eileen?

EILEEN. Nothin'. I'm just finishin' off a bit of work, that's all.

MOLLY. Of a Sunday night! I thought there was someone after breakin' into the place or somethin'.

MOLLY *lights up a cigarette.*

EILEEN. Were yeh over in Larkin's Molly?

MOLLY. Yeah.

EILEEN. Is me Daddy over there?

MOLLY. Yes he is. He's in right form over there. There's a great stave altogether goin' on. Young Lugs McGuire has the guitar out and everythin'. I had three or four drinks meself this evenin'. I don't know who was buyin' 'em nor nothin'. I drank 'em anyway Eileen. To hell with the lot of them. If we had lost the match today we would have had to listen to them all moanin' for the next fortnight.

EILEEN. Is Georgie there?

MOLLY. That's what I was just goin' to say to yeh. Georgie Whelan sang, 'One Way Love' over there tonight and I swear to God Eileen it was only beautiful. They tore the place down for him so they did. And then Lugs McGuire sang the song that he made up about Red O'Neill. Ah yeh should hear it. It's great. He's after addin' another verse to it about all the lads who were on the bus goin' up to the match. Your Da and everyone is mentioned. Little Mickey Morris is doin' his nut because it kind of insinuates that himself and Big Mag Delaney 'll be gettin' engaged shortly. And Joe! – ah be Jaysus Joe bet the bun altogether. He sang 'I gave my wedding dress away', which he dedicated to Big Mag who of course was engaged about three times before. Joe said that she ruptured the first two fellas and the third lad got sense.

MOLLY *laughs.* EILEEN *is unmoved.* MOLLY *spies the suitcase.*

Well what did yeh think of the other fella comin' home?

EILEEN. Who's that?

MOLLY. Danger Doyle! Ah now Eileen, don't try and tell me that yeh never knew he was back.

EILEEN. Oh I knew he was back alright.

MOLLY. By Jaysus he has some neck on him though Eileen hasn't he? As brazen as yeh please, he comes waltzin' into the street yesterday, a great suit and tie and him and all. I thought it was Montgomery Clift or someone for a minute. 'How are yeh honey bunch?', says he to me, a fancy twang in his voice. He's stoppin' down in the County Hotel I believe. I suppose none of his own would have him. He was supposed to come into Larkin's for a few drinks this evenin' but he never showed up. He must have had more important things to do I suppose . . . So what are yeh goin' to do Eileen?

EILEEN. I don't know.

MOLLY. I'd stay well clear of him if I were you hon. Take it from one who knows and let him go back to where he came from because he's trouble with a capital T that fella is. Yes, a capital T.

EILEEN. Do yeh not think he's changed Molly?

MOLLY. Changed? People don't change Eileen. Not really. Underneath they stay the same . . . Yeh know sometimes you really remind me of your Mammy. The way yeh looked at me that time now – so secretive or somethin'. I don't know what it was about her but she always seemed to know somethin' that we didn't. Some little thing that set her apart from the rest of us. Somethin' so simple that it must have been starin' me right in the face, only I could never for the life of me figure out what it was. I wouldn't mind but I always felt that if I had been able to crack it I could have been somebody in this town. But I never did. I never found out what it was that set her apart. You're lucky Eileen. I was often watchin' yeh walkin' down the street. Or comin' out of Byrne's Café with Johnny Doran or someone. You get that confidence from your Mammy. I've only felt like that once in me life. It was a few years ago now. I took a good look in the mirror and I was surprised to find that I liked what I saw there. So I primped meself up and went to pay a call on this lonely man I know – because let's face it if a woman can't help to mend a broken heart then what the hell's the point of it all. Well, his face dropped when he opened the door and saw me standin' there. I told him out straight what I had come for. 'Go Away' he said and he shut the door in me face. (*She laughs.*) Huh, some of us have it is right! I bet nobody 'll ever shut a door in your face, Eileen.

MOLLY *looks blatantly down at the suitcase and then back at* EILEEN.

You're worse Eileen, havin' anything to do with him.

EILEEN. Ah he's alright. I'm sure he's not the worst of them.

MOLLY. Look Eileen, you don't know him. I know him. I know all belongin' to him. He never worked a day in his life. He wouldn't work in a fit. I'm tellin' yeh you're better off stayin' well away from him altogether. Anyway ain't yeh grand and snug where yeh are, with your own little room and your records and all without gettin' involved with the likes of him.

STEVEN *enters.*

EILEEN. Hello Daddy.

STEVEN. Eileen.

MOLLY. Steven there 'll vouch for that now . . . Georgie Whelan singin' 'One Way Love'. Beautiful Steven, wasn't it?

STEVEN. Yeah.

MOLLY. He has a grand voice, hasn't he?

STEVEN. Yeah. He's a nice singer alright.

MOLLY. I was just tellin' Eileen about it here. And did yeh hear the song Lugs McGuire made up? What was the part in it about you Steven?

EILEEN. Did you get anythin' to eat today Daddy?

STEVEN. Yeah I had a bowl of soup and a few sandwiches earlier on.

MOLLY. Steven Redmond let out a roar or somethin' wasn't it?

EILEEN (*going behind the partition*). Huh, you'll get fat on that.

MOLLY. No. Steven Redmond let out a shout though.

STEVEN. What's goin' on Eileen?

MOLLY (*sings*).
  Steven Redmond let out a shout
  Oh says he there is no doubt . . .

EILEEN. I'll tell yeh after Daddy.

MOLLY (*sings*).
  That Red O'Neill is . . .

 But sure I don't suppose you ever found out what it was
 that set her apart either Steven did yeh?

STEVEN. What?

MOLLY. Eileen! I danced with your Da one time in the
  Town Hall yeh know. It was a New Year's Eve dance. The
  place was covered with decorations, mistletoe over the
  door and all. You don't remember that Steven, do yeh?
  Meself and Joe came second in the Rock and Roll
  competition that night. Little Mickey Morris and big Mag
  Delaney won it. I had these big earrings on me and a real
  tight skirt. It was a lady's choice and I asked your Da up
  for it. He don't remember that of course. Do yeh?

STEVEN. I remember it alright.

MOLLY (*singing*). Kiss me honey, honey kiss me.

STEVEN. But sure that was the first time I ever asked her
  up to dance.

MOLLY. Thrill me honey honey thrill me . . .

STEVEN. Take Good Care Of My Baby!

MOLLY. Don't care even if I blow my top but honey
  honey . . .

STEVEN. My hand on the small of her back.

MOLLY. We ended up under the mistletoe Eileen. For all
  the good it done me! I'm not coddin' yeh he was like an
  auld sour grape in my arms now, the same fella. Yes, a
  sour grape you were like boy!

  JOE *and* GEORGIE *enter, arms around each other and singing. They
  are wearing team sashes and hats and scarves etc.*

JOE and GEORGIE (*sing*).
> Oh the Wayward Wind is a restless wind
> A restless wind that yearns to wander
> And I was born the next of kin
> The next of kin to the Wayward Wind.

MOLLY *joins in with the singing. She waltzes around the place, dancing over to* STEVEN *and forcing him to dance with her.* EILEEN *emerges to see her father abruptly breaking away from* MOLLY's *grasp.* JOE *is using a stick of rock as a microphone.*

MOLLY. What's wrong with yeh Steven? Jaysus you're as miserable. No wonder your missus ran off on yeh.

MOLLY *goes and joins* GEORGIE *and* JOE *in song. She takes the scarf from* GEORGIE *and drapes it around her own neck.*

GEORGIE, JOE *and* MOLLY (*sing*).
> In a lonely shack by a railroad track
> I spent my younger days
> And I guess the sound of the outward bound
> Made me a slave to my wandering ways.

JOE *breaks away while the others keep singing.*

JOE. Well Steven, what did yeh think of that then?

STEVEN. What's that?

JOE. Today! What did yeh think of it?

STEVEN. God, it was a right day.

JOE (*passionately*). Yeah but what did yeh think of it though? Did we do it or not? Yes or no?

STEVEN. Ah we did it alright.

JOE. Hah? Put it there me auld flower, we hurled 'em out of it so we did. Did yeh ever in all your born days Steven see anythin' like that last goal that Big Red O'Neill scored. Be the Lord Harry tonight, he buried it into the back of the net and that's all's about it.

GEORGIE. A beautiful goal.

JOE. What?

GEORGIE. It was a beautiful goal and I don't care what anyone says about it.

JOE. Beautiful! I'm goin' to tell yeh one thing here and now for nothin' boy but that was a classic goal so it was. They'll be debatin' and discussin' that goal for a queer long time to come you mark my words. Am I right or am I wrong Steven?

STEVEN *nods.*

GEORGIE. It was a deadly goal alright, no doubt about it.

JOE. Deadly! Meself and Mickey Morris kissed and hugged one another so hard that people started wonderin' about us, that's how deadly it was. Yes, you're livin' in the greatest little town in Ireland so yeh are boy and yeh don't even realise it. Put it there Steven, we hurled 'em out of it, so we did.

They shake hands. JOE *spies* MOLLY *eyeing them scornfully.*

Hey Steven, what would yeh think of a one who wouldn't even cheer for her own home town on the day of the All Ireland Final? What would yeh do with her eh . . .? Wouldn't even support her own flesh and blood. I don't know. Ah sure, what harm. We did it without her anyway.

GEORGIE *yelps.*

MOLLY. What do yeh mean 'we'? I didn't hear your name gettin' called out on the television or anythin'.

JOE. What did yeh say?

MOLLY. You heard me.

JOE. I didn't hear yeh. What did yeh say?

MOLLY. How many goals did you score today . . . How many balls did Georgie there put over the bar? The way you're talkin' anyone 'd think that you had somethin' to do with Big Red's goal. You had nothin' to do with it boy. Big Red O'Neill scored the goal all by himself.

JOE. I was there to cheer him on anyway. More than you were.

MOLLY. You had nothin' to do with it.

STEVEN. That's where you're wrong girl.

JOE. What do yeh mean I had nothin' to do with it?

STEVEN. No one man can . . .

JOE. I'm a Wexfordman and he's a Wexfordman.

MOLLY. So?

STEVEN. . . . achieve what a whole team can achieve. No one individual can . . .

JOE. So it's the same thing. When he scores I score. Or we score I should say.

MOLLY. Ah will yeh go away out of that and don't be annoyin' yourself Joe.

STEVEN. . . . even hope to whatdoyoucallit . . .

JOE. I wouldn't expect you to understand Molly.

STEVEN. I've been goin' to hurlin' matches for a queer long time now and if there's one thing that I've . . .

JOE. It's beyond your comprehension girl. You're worse than Steven.

STEVEN. What?

JOE. Sure that one wouldn't know her arse from her elbow now regardin' hurlin'.

MOLLY. I know as much as you about it I'd say.

JOE. Yes yeh do yeah. Look Molly yeh might as well admit it, yeh don't know the first thing about it.

MOLLY. Yeah well, maybe I don't know a whole lot about it but I'll tell yeh one thing I do know though. Big Red O'Neill must be browned off carryin' you crowd of ejits on his back everywhere he goes. It's a wonder some of yeh wouldn't get down and walk a bit of the way once in a while.

JOE. Hey, there's no man ever had to carry me on his back nor ever will either. No one had to carry me into Croke Park this afternoon. I walked in there of me own free will. (MOLLY *scoffs*.) Yeh see the trouble with you Molly is yeh have no time for this town. Well I have because I happen to believe that a man without a hometown is nothin'. Am I right or am I wrong Steven?

STEVEN. That's right. A man without a hometown is nothin'. He's lost.

JOE. Now yeh said it Steven. Lost is right. In the wilderness he is.

MOLLY. Are you two gone soft in the head or what? I mean what's this town ever done for any of you, only laughed at yez.

JOE. Hey, this town, nor nobody in it for that matter, has ever laughed at me mate.

MOLLY. They laughed at yeh. And do yeh want to know why?

JOE. No one in this town has ever laughed at me.

MOLLY. Well I'll tell yeh why. Because for the past ten years you've been like an auld chicken without a head runnin' around the place – organisin' this and organisin' that.

JOE. I wasn't the only one that Danger left behind Molly.

MOLLY. No but you're the one who does most of the bullshittin' about him every chance yeh get. (*Pause.*) Huh, next you'll be tryin' to tell me that nobody has ever laughed at Steven there either.

STEVEN. I'll have you know that I've never done anythin' in this town to be ashamed of.

MOLLY. Yeh must have a queer bad memory then Steven.

STEVEN. What do yeh mean?

MOLLY. Your name was scrawled all over half the walls of the town man. *Steven Redmond is a eunuch.* Do yeh not remember that one Steven? Well I do. And *Ole King Cole lives in a brothel.* Georgie did that one. Yeah, good old Georgie.

JOE. You're out of order now Molly.

MOLLY. Who the hell do you think yeh are anyway Steven, goin' around shuttin' doors in people's faces and walkin' around with your nose in the air. Jaysus Christ man anyone'd think that you had . . .

JOE. You're way out of order girl.

MOLLY. Ah go and fuck off Joe will yeh.

MOLLY *retreats to a corner.*

STEVEN. I don't see why I have to stand here in me own hometown and listen to this kind of talk. I mean to say I've never done anything to be . . .

STEVEN *sees the suitcase for the first time. He looks from it to* EILEEN. *Stunned, he looks around him at the others like a bereaved man and then he goes and sits at the table in the anteroom.*

EILEEN (*furious, going to* MOLLY). There was no need to rear up on him like that.

MOLLY. Yes there was. I'm sick and tired of him lookin' down his nose at me.

EILEEN. What do yeh mean?

MOLLY. He looks down his nose at me all the time, turnin' away when he meets me in the street and all. Jaysus, he wouldn't even give us a feckin' auld dance at the factory reunion last year.

EILEEN. So what? He ought to kiss your feet every time he meets yeh now.

MOLLY. Look Eileen, you're not the one who feels like a piece of dirt every time he turns to look at yeh. Anyone 'd think I had done somethin' on him. It's not my fault that your Ma cleared off to England. If he had 've been man enough in the first place to hang on to her he wouldn't be in this predicament now.

EILEEN. You're only takin' it out on him because Danger is back in town and because he came back for me and not for you.

MOLLY. That has nothin' to do with it. I wouldn't touch Danger Doyle nor anythin' belongin' to him now with a forty foot pole.

EILEEN. Oh yeah, pull the other one Molly. You laugh about me Daddy's name appearin' on half the walls of the town but if the truth be told you'd have given your right arm once upon a time for your name to be up there too. Danger and Molly in the middle of a great big heart or somethin'. And now yeh have the nerve to make out that Danger was never anything but a dirty corner boy and yeh talk about me Mammy as if she was just another little workin' class bitch in heat. Well you'd want to take a good look at your own poxy life Molly before yeh go tearin' strips off of other people's.

EILEEN *walks away, down the steps and across to the counter.*

GEORGIE. Well said Eileen. By Jaysus you're well able to fight your corner alright. Ain't she Joe?

JOE. What?

GEORGIE. I say she's well able to stand up for herself.

EILEEN *throws him a contemptuous look.* JOE *hushes him up.* GEORGIE *goes to* EILEEN.

Yeh know somethin' Eileen, this has certainly been an enlightenin' few days alright hasn't it? – between one thing and another.

EILEEN. What do yeh mean?

GEORGIE. Well I mean to say you found out somethin' about me and I found out somethin' about you . . .

EILEEN. You found out somethin' about me? What? What was it?

GEORGIE. Ain't that right Joe?

JOE. What?

GEORGIE. I say we found out a lot about ourselves in the past few days.

JOE. Feckin' right we did. We hurled 'em out of it that's all.

EILEEN. Georgie, what did you find out about me?

GEORGIE. What?

EILEEN. What did yeh find out about me?

GEORGIE. Let's just say that I happened to overhear someone mention that famous afternoon you and the carnival boy spent in your house while your Da was away at a match somewhere.

EILEEN. What about it?

GEORGIE. How the pair of yeh slipped off hand in hand down to the bedroom when no one was lookin'.

EILEEN. Yeah well it wasn't quite like that Georgie.

GEORGIE. Oh yeah. And what was it quite like then?

EILEEN. Ah it doesn't matter now.

GEORGIE. Yes it does matter. It matters to me anyway. I've known you for as long as I can remember and in all that time I've never even tried to . . .

EILEEN. What?

GEORGIE. You must have had a right laugh about me did yeh – you and him?

EILEEN. Georgie I've never laughed at you in me life. I've laughed with yeh and about yeh but I've never laughed at yeh.

GEORGIE. Yeh must have. I mean while I was hangin' around here all the time, gettin' sweet nothin' off of you, you were . . .

EILEEN. I was what? Look Georgie, it was never supposed to be like that between you and me.

GEORGIE. Yeah well let's face it, you weren't exactly what you were lettin' on to be were yeh?

EILEEN *throws her eyes to heaven.*

I don't like anyone tryin' to gull me Eileen.

EILEEN. Sure God help yeh, you're killed aren't yeh? Jaysus, and I thought I could depend on you.

GEORGIE. Yeah well, that was before I found out what you were made of wasn't it? That was before I found out that you were just like your Ma – a real skeet goin' around.

EILEEN. What are yeh tryin' to do boy, scorch the ground from in under us or somethin'?

GEORGIE. You're the one who's done the scorchin' Eileen, not me. For the past few days my heart's been down in my shoes or somewhere over you girl . . . Yeh keep me hangin' on all the time Eileen so that I don't know whether I'm comin' or goin' with yeh. I mean I don't know what I'm supposed to do. What am I supposed to do?

EILEEN. I'm sorry, Georgie. I didn't know yeh felt like that. It was never supposed to be like that between you and me.

GEORGIE. Ah forget about it. I don't think you'll be seein' a whole lot of me around here any more anyway. I wouldn't lower meself to tell yeh nothin' but the truth.

GEORGIE *turns away from her.* EILEEN *is saddened. She reaches under the counter and takes the record out. She leaves it on the counter in front of him and she goes off to the office.* GEORGIE *turns to watch her go. He picks up the record and begins to smash it off of the edge of the counter.*

JOE. What's the matter Georgie? What's up?

GEORGIE. Hey Joe, remember what you were sayin' the other day about Eileen.

JOE. What?

GEORGIE. Eileen!

JOE. What about her?

GEORGIE. Remember what you were sayin' about her?

MOLLY. What ails him?

JOE. He's alright. A bit too much to drink that's all. He'll be alright.

GEORGIE (*gripping* JOE). Listen to me Joe, will yeh. This is important.

JOE. What's wrong with yeh?

GEORGIE. I need to know if what you were sayin' about Eileen the other day is . . .

JOE. Forget about Eileen, Georgie will yeh.

GEORGIE. What?

JOE. Forget about her.

JOE *frees himself from* GEORGIE's *grip and breaks away.* GEORGIE *plonks himself down on the bench.*

Young fellas!

JOE *goes up into the anteroom. He takes a naggon of whisky from his coat pocket.*

Do you want a drop of whisky Steven?

STEVEN *shakes his head.* JOE *goes in behind the counter and down into the office. He returns with two cups and he begins to pour out some whisky. He hands one of the cups to* MOLLY. *He takes a slug himself and then he holds his cup aloft and sings.*

JOE (*sings*).
    I want to be your lover.
    But your friend is all I stay
    You leave me halfway to Paradise
    So near, yet so far away.

Do you remember that one Molly? You, me and Danger down in Byrne's Café, knockin' back the Coca Cola, me and Danger dressed up to kill in a couple of suits we just bought on the never never. Yeh know I was often thinkin' Molly that if Danger hadn't come along when he did you and me would've nearly . . .

MOLLY. What? You and me would've never nearly nothin'. Sure you were never any good with women.

JOE. Hey, I knew me onions when it came to women mate.

MOLLY. Yeh never had any way with women.

JOE. And what about June Carty? And young Whitney? Or Big

Mag Delaney? Or that young one used to live on the corner of King street there. The litany of women goes on and on I don't mind tellin' yeh. And when I'd get on the little football table the whole place'd flock around me because I was a bit of a shark at that game. You ask Danger. Even he used to bow to me boy.

MOLLY. Pocket billiards 'd be more like it I'd say.

JOE. And what about those two English girls who came home here one summer. One of them was dyin' alive about me.

MOLLY. Yeah and you spent the whole summer threatenin' to ask her to go to the pictures with yeh, so that in the end Mickey Morris asked her out and that was that.

JOE. I asked her out.

MOLLY. Yes yeh did, yeah!

GEORGIE *begins to cough and splutter as he makes for the door.*

JOE. Good man Georgie. Get it up out of yeh me auld son.

JOE *looks at* GEORGIE *and laughs. He pours some more whisky into* MOLLY's *cup and toasts.*

JOE. Anyway Molly, here's to Red O'Neill and the sportin' life.

MOLLY. What the hell would you know about the sportin' life? A hurler on the ditch is all you ever were.

JOE. And what's wrong with that? Someone has to stand on the sidelines and keep the auld thing goin' yeh know. We all can't be Red O'Neill's or anythin' . . . Lose yourself in the crowd Molly, that's my motto.

MOLLY. Yeah I know. But then you're probably hidin' from the fact that yeh once turned your back on your best friend just when he needed yeh the most. And then yeh had the nerve to laugh at him when he cried.

JOE (*sadly*). Only out of relief Molly because he didn't give me away . . . He didn't give me away.

MOLLY. Yeah well, don't worry about it Joe. He made up for it in the end. He betrayed the whole shaggin' lot of us.

JOE. No, you're wrong there Molly. Danger Doyle never betrayed no one in this town.

MOLLY. Ah.

GEORGIE *returns*.

JOE. I'm goin' to tell yeh one thing Molly here and now for nothin' because it's high time that this whole thing was whatdoyoucallit . . .

MOLLY. You're drunk.

JOE. What?

MOLLY. Go away from me will yeh.

JOE. I'm not drunk. Listen to me. I was Danger's best mate and I didn't even know he was goin' to run away. I was drinkin' with him the night before he went and he didn't even tell me. And I was his best mate. But he didn't betray me. Yeh can't say that he betrayed me.

GEORGIE. Hey Joe, he's no use boy. He's no friggin' use.

MOLLY. Now yeh said it Georgie. He's no use is right. He's a dead bloody loss so he is. And then he comes home and you fellas roll out the red carpet for him. I'd like me job now.

GEORGIE. There's no welcome on my mat for him anyway, Molly. Nor for anyone belongin' to him either.

JOE. Ah that's a load of balls Georgie.

GEORGIE. There's no need to stand up for him all the time Joe.

JOE. I'm not standin' up for him Georgie. I'm just sayin' that's all.

Pause.

MOLLY. Yes, I'd like me job.

Pause.

JOE. There's a thing I was just thinkin' of today though Molly. About the time Danger got that job workin' on the bumpers above in that auld fairground remember? And he used to let you and me go on 'em for nothin' all the time. My jeans were so tight that I nearly did meself a mischief one night climbin' down off the merry-go-round. Oh the pain of it! 'Sealed with a Kiss', blarin' out over the big loudspeakers.

(*Sings.*) Oh it's gonna be a long lonely summer . . .
By Jaysus it very nearly was too.

Pause.

MOLLY. You always played sad songs on the jukebox.

A wild cheer outside and a host of voices singing, 'One Way Love', to a simple guitar accompaniment.

JOE. There's your auld song now, Georgie.

JOE goes to the door.

GEORGIE. What can yeh do with a girl like that Joe eh? I mean what are yeh supposed to do with her?

JOE. Forget about her Georgie. Because yeh might as well be pissin' against the wind as to wish for somethin' yeh can't have. Am I right or am I wrong Molly?

MOLLY. Some people are born to be hurt, some to do the hurtin'. It's as simple as that. That's just the nature of things.

JOE. Come on and we'll all go out around the auld bonfire and have a bit of a singsong Molly. Come on. Are yeh comin' out Georgie?

GEORGIE. Naw.

JOE. Come on out of that.

JOE leaves just as EILEEN comes out of the office. GEORGIE looks at her and then guiltily turns away. MOLLY is sitting in the alcove of the bay window. EILEEN looks out through the little window behind the counter.

VOICES (*singing*).
While you're up there and I'm sinking fast
You must be living in a plastercast
I don't think I'm gonna last my whole life through
With you . . .

DANGER DOYLE *enters.*

VOICES (*singing*).
One way love.
One way love.

The song ends and a great cheer goes up around the bonfire.

DANGER. How are yeh Eileen?

EILEEN. Hello.

DANGER. Is that your case? (EILEEN *nods.*) There's a taxi waitin' across the street to take us down to the harbour.

Pause.

EILEEN. I'll get me coat.

She goes down to the office. Silence as DANGER *looks from* MOLLY *to* GEORGIE *to* STEVEN. *A wild cheer outside.*

DANGER. I'd say there was a good auld atmosphere up at the match today Molly was there?

MOLLY. I don't know. I wasn't at it meself. You'd want to ask Steven about that . . . Anyway I didn't think you'd have any interest in it one way or another.

DANGER. Ah yeah. I was watchin' it on the box down in the hotel this afternoon. The camera panned in on the crowd there at one stage. I thought sure we'd catch a glimpse of one of the boys – Mickey Morris or someone.

MOLLY. But sure they're all outside now standing around the bonfire if you're wantin' to go and shake hands with any of them . . . (DANGER *shrugs.*) Go and climb down off of your high horse there mister. Who the hell do yeh think yeh are anyway?

DANGER. To tell yeh the truth Molly I'm half afraid to climb down in case I end up like your man whatshisname . . . Oisín. Do yeh remember that story? He came back from a place called Tír Na Nóg and as soon as he touched the ground he turned into an auld fella. I'll never forget the first mornin' the Christian Brother told us about that and I remember thinkin' at the time that a man'd want to be a bit soft in the head or somethin' to come back from a land of eternal youth just because he wanted to see his auld mates again. . . He must have had somethin' else on his mind Molly, hah?

MOLLY. Yeah.

JOE (*enters, laughing hysterically*). Little Mickey Morris is after gettin' so sick out there that he nearly put out the fire . . . Hey Georgie, come on they're wantin' you to sing a song out here . . . Oh be Jaysus look at Danger where he is. Hey, this one was blackguardin' the lot of us here today Danger.

DANGER. Among yeh be it, Joe.

JOE. What?

MOLLY. He said he don't want any part in the discussion. And who could blame the man. Anyone who runs away with a circus is hardly goin' to come back to see an auld sideshow now is he?

JOE. Did yeh go up to the match after Danger?

DANGER. No.

JOE. That's a pity. You should have come up on the bus with us. Yeh could have had your name mentioned in young Lugs McGuire's song now.

MOLLY. That man has no desire to be swallowed up by the crowd like you yeh know Joe. He wants a song all to himself. Don't yeh Danger?

JOE. It wouldn't be the first time meself and Danger had songs written about us.

DANGER. Yeah but I think we made most of them up ourselves though Joe.

JOE. So what have yeh been up to since yeh got back?

DANGER. Ah I don't know. Just takin' a good look round really.

MOLLY. What, from your hotel window yeh mean?

DANGER. I went into Byrne's Café today.

MOLLY (*testily*). What for?

  DANGER *shrugs*.

DANGER. I see the auld jukebox is still goin' strong down there anyway.

JOE. Yeah, still pumpin' away down there. I'm goin' to tell yeh one thing boy but they don't make 'em like that no more. So what did yeh think of the place? Still the same ain't it? Nothin' changes boy . . . Jaysus we had some good times together though Danger, didn't we? Remember the day yeh cut the arse off of yourself gettin' out over the nun's wall. And the time yeh climbed up to the top of the chapel to hang your hat on the steeple. I'm not coddin' yeh boy but yeh nearly put the heart crossways in me that day lookin' at yeh. I must have had half your obituary written before yeh came back down . . . So what are yeh at over there this weather anyway Danger?

DANGER. I'm workin' in a car factory. Auld shift work.

JOE. I thought you were still with the cigarette people.

DANGER. No. I got sacked out of there for being overweight one night . . . five or six cartons overweight.

DANGER *grins.* JOE *thinks about it and laughs.*

JOE. Still the same auld Danger . . . Hey do yeh know who I
bumped into the other day? That country girl that you walked
home from a dance one night. Remember yeh walked about
seven miles out into the country with her and she didn't even
give yeh a good night kiss.

DANGER. I walked seven miles. Joe, you were the one who walked
her home not me.

JOE. Ah come on now Danger, don't try and turn the tables on
me. I remember you talkin' about the blisters on your feet the
next day.

DANGER. The blisters on your feet yeh mean.

MOLLY. Oh for God's sake. Look if you two are goin' to kiss the
past's arse all night long then I wish the pair of yeh would go
somewhere else and do it.

JOE. What's wrong with you?

MOLLY. Yeh haven't seen each other in nearly ten years! Don't
yeh have nothin' important to say to one another? Isn't there
anythin' to forgive? Isn't there somethin' to forget?

JOE. The only thing meself and Danger have to say to one another
is that we had some good times together. There's nothin' to
either forgive or to forget. Ain't that right Danger?

DANGER. That's right Joe. Nothin' that time hasn't washed away
by now anyway Molly.

MOLLY. Want to bet.

JOE. Ordinarily he means Molly. With ordinary people.

MOLLY. What's that supposed to mean?

JOE. It's a joke.

MOLLY. Oh stop. Sure you're a real Groucho Marx goin' around
with your jokes.

She turns away. Pause.

JOE. We must take a bit of a stroll together around some of the
auld haunts one day Danger, now that you're here. I'm goin' to
tell yeh one thing boy but you won't believe some of the changes
that are after . . .

EILEEN *enters, a small overnight case in her hand, her overcoat on.*
DANGER*'s gaze wanders towards her, stopping* JOE *in his tracks. All
eyes are on* EILEEN *now.*

MOLLY (*toasting*). Welcome to the ranks of the left behind
Georgie.

JOE. Are yeh off Danger?

DANGER *nods.*

I thought yeh were hangin' around for a while?

DANGER. I have to get back to work Joe like, yeh know.

Pause. JOE *indicates that he understands. He goes to* DANGER.

JOE. Well put it there me auld stock. (*They shake hands.*) And don't
leave it so long the next time will yeh? Because before yeh know
it they'll be plantin' one or the other of us in the ground so they
will.

DANGER. Yeah, see yeh Joe.

JOE. And another thing, we broke into this place more than twice.
It was five or six times at the very least and I won't have you
sayin' anythin' to the contrary boy . . . And listen, I did whistle
out to yeh that night, Danger. I know you said yeh never heard
me and all but I whistled out to yeh. I swear.

Silence as the two men stare into each other's eyes. Then JOE *breaks
away, winks and leaves.* DANGER *watches the empty doorway.*
MOLLY *approaches.*

MOLLY. And I called out your name that day up in the courtroom
when I saw yeh standin' there with the tears in your eyes.

DANGER. I never heard yeh.

MOLLY. That's because it was kind of soft and low, Danger.

GEORGIE *laughs.*

What's so funny?

GEORGIE. Danger Doyle, the big hard man cryin' his eyes out up
in the courtroom.

GEORGIE *rises and laughing manically he stumbles across to*
DANGER.

Cryin' his eyes out up in the courtroom he was. Danger Doyle,
the big hard man.

GEORGIE *leaves shouting at the top of his voice all over the street.*
EILEEN, *concerned goes to look out the little window.*

The big famous Danger Doyle cryin' like a baby up in the
courtroom . . . (*He laughs manically.*)

DANGER. That's it Georgie boy, you shout it from the rooftops
son.

MOLLY. What did you want to come back here for anyway? As if I
wasn't tangled up enough already without havin' to see you
again.

DANGER. I just came back to kiss the cross they hung me on
Molly. Or maybe I came back to set you free.

MOLLY. Free? To do what? To go where?

Slight pause.

DANGER. To stay here?

MOLLY. Oh and I suppose we're all expected to be eternally
grateful to the great Danger Doyle for settin' us free are we?
Well let me tell you one thing Mister, here and now for nothin',
but I don't need you nor any other fella like yeh either to set me
free. I don't need you to . . .

It is the calmness and tenderness in DANGER's *eyes that stops her from
going on. She backs away to gaze lovingly at his face. Pause.*

Aw Danger . . . Doyle if you only knew! Yeh know when you ran
away with her like that I kept tellin' meself that it wouldn't last,
that it wouldn't be long until yeh came back again to me. I'd
picture yeh strollin' into town, kickin' up the leaves, your hair
fallin' down into your eyes the way it used to and I'd be smilin'
away to meself at the very idea of it – in spite of the fact that
there was a great big knot screwin' and twistin' inside of me all
the time. After a while of course it all turned kind of sour so that
in the end, I'm not coddin' yeh, I felt like some poor beast that
had been left out too long in the rain. Yeh'd forgotten me yeh
see. Yeh'd forgotten all about me.

DANGER. No Molly, I never forgot yeh hon. Never. Yeh know
you were the first girl ever to make me feel half decent in this
town and I'll always remember yeh for it. But that was a long
time ago Molly and you can search me if yeh want but I swear to
God I don't have what you seem to think I took from yeh.

Silence.

MOLLY. What am I goin' to do Danger?

He has no answer. Pause.

I'll see yeh.

DANGER. Yeah . . . see yeh Molly.

MOLLY *leaves.*

EILEEN. I've never seen Georgie like this before. Maybe I should go out to him.

DANGER. Leave him alone Eileen. He'll be alright. Who knows with a bit of luck he might wind up washin' my name away for once and for all . . . Are you alright?

EILEEN *nods. Pause.* DANGER *turns to* STEVEN.

I'm terrible sorry about the way things turned out Steven. I never meant to . . . Well I'm sorry about the way things went.

EILEEN. Danger says that me Mammy misses me terrible Daddy and that she's dyin' to see me again. I'm goin' to go back with him for a little while.

DANGER. She's a bit down in herself at the moment over there, Steven like, yeh know. I just felt that it might do her good to see Eileen again.

EILEEN. It's just for a while Daddy.

Pause.

STEVEN. And I thought I was goin' to sneak through life unnoticed . . . This town'll be the death of me yet.

STEVEN *rises and goes across to look out of the bay window.*

God I hate to see anybody carryin' a suitcase – anyone belongin' to me anyway. Would yeh believe it Eileen but I've never packed a bag in me life. Just sleepin' in Dublin last night now nearly put years on me. I can't understand why people can't stay put. I mean what's the attraction out there anyway? Everyone keeps reachin' for the moon. I wouldn't mind but half of them wouldn't even know what to do with it if it fell into their laps. It seems to be a mortal sin these days to want to stay where yeh are . . . Your Mammy was the very same. She was always wonderin' what was over the next hill. She was always wonderin' about somethin'. Jukebox fellas and carnival boys seemed to fascinate her. A fancy scarf blowin' in the wind, a tattoo, anythin'

the least bit outlandish at all and she was off. I never knew
whether I was comin' or goin' with her. I never really knew what
way I was fixed with her at all to tell yeh the truth.

Pause.

EILEEN. I have to go to her Daddy. I mean if she's not goin' to
come to me then I have to go to her don't I?

STEVEN *plonks himself down sadly into the alcove of the bay window.
Outside the crowd are singing 'The Girl Of My Best Friend'.*

VOICES (*singing.*)
  The way she walks
  The way she talks
  How long can I pretend . . .

EILEEN. Don't I Daddy?

STEVEN *sighs and then nods in agreement. Pause.*

DANGER. I'll stick this out in the boot of the car Eileen.

DANGER *takes the suitcase and heads towards the door. He stops in the
doorway.*

She's still terrible fond of you, yeh know Steven. She'd never let
anyone say nothin' against yeh now nor nothin'.

Pause. DANGER *leaves. Silence except for the singing outside.*

STEVEN. I never meant to hinder yeh from seein' your Mammy
or anythin' Eileen yeh know. Nor her from seein' you for that
matter . . . It seems she more or less regarded me as some sort of
an auld snare that she was all caught up in so while she had the
chance she was goin' to make a run for it. In a taxi down to the
harbour with Danger Doyle! It was all in the note that I found
on top of me lunch box that mornin' – in her little dainty
handwritin' . . . It broke my heart when she ran off on me like
that yeh know. It broke me bloody heart so it did.

STEVEN *hangs his head sadly.* EILEEN *stands motionless, her eyes
brimming with tears.* STEVEN *rises and braces himself.*

Are yeh alright for money?

EILEEN. Yeah, I've enough money . . . I'll write to yeh as soon as I
get there.

STEVEN. Aye, do.

EILEEN. Will yeh be able to manage alright here Daddy?

STEVEN. Yeah.

EILEEN (*going to him*). Goodbye Daddy.

They embrace. She breaks away and leaves. Pause.

STEVEN *looks around the shop.*

VOICES (*outside, singing*).
Will My Aching Heart never mend
Oh will I always be in love
With the girl of my best friend . . .

Lights down.

BELFRY

Belfry was produced for television by Initial Film and Television and first screened on BBC-2 in summer 1993 as part of *The Wexford Trilogy*. The cast was as follows:

ANGELA	Ingrid Craigie
DOMINIC	Aidan Gillen
FATHER PAT	Gary Lydon
ARTIE O'LEARY	Des McAleer
DONAL	Michael O'Hagan

Directed by Stuart Burge, produced by Emma Burge and designed by Christine Edzard at the Sands Films studios in Rotherhithe.

Belfry was first staged at the Bush Theatre, London on 13 November, 1991. Press night was on 18 November 1991. The cast was as follows:-

ANGELA	Ingrid Craigie
DOMINIC	Aidan Gillen
FATHER PAT	Gary Lydon
ARTIE O'LEARY	Des McAleer
DONAL	Michael O'Hagan

Directed by Robin Lefevre
Designed by Andrew Wood
Lighting by Tina MacHugh
Sound by John Leonard

Characters

ANGELA
DOMINIC
FATHER PAT
ARTIE O'LEARY
DONAL

Setting

The stage is divided into two sections. The main area is the belfry – a dusty place with bare floorboards. There is a stack of chimes to the back and in the shadows a door. There are two windows – a small one looking down into the chapel and a large stained glass window which looks down onto the street. Upstage there is a rope dangling from the ceiling and centre stage there is a big basket which is choc-a-bloc with old vestments and garments and old bunting, etc. A second door seems to lead further up into the tower of the church.

The second section is the vestry. This is a well-ordered carpeted room which is equipped with all the usual paraphernalia that can be found in a place of this sort. There are three doors – one leading to the chapel, one to the street and another small door leads into a little closet room where the coats and vestments are kept. There is a long bench by the street door and a small table and chairs upstage.

The play is set in Wexford, a small town in Ireland.

ACT ONE

Lights up on the belfry. ARTIE *is sitting on the basket.*

ARTIE (*to the audience*). I know what they think of me. I know well
enough what they say about me behind my back. There he goes,
Artie O'Leary the poor little sacristan with the candle grease on
his sleeve, smellin' of incense as he opens the big heavy belfry
door. They watch me standin' quietly in the shadows of the
mortuary when they come to bury their dead and they see me
goin' home to my little empty house in the rain every night to
listen to the news. Lonely auld days and nights they're thinkin'.
Dreary auld mornings too. Snuffin' out candles and emptyin'
poor boxes. Of course they've all probably forgotten by now that
I once loved a woman. Another man's wife. She came into this
queer auld whisperin' world of mine to change the flowers in the
chapel and to look after the altar and although she's been gone
out of here over a year now I swear to God her fragrance still
lingers about the place – in the transept, near the shrine.
Around the vestry and above in the belfry – her scent . . . where
ever I go . . . It's thanks to her that I have a past worth talkin'
about at all I suppose. Although I often curse her for it. There
are days now when I find myself draggin' her memory behind
me everywhere I go. I bless her too though. She tapped a hidden
reservoir inside of me that I didn't even know was there.

Because of her I now find myself ramblin' into snooker halls and
back room card games where, surrounded by archin' eyebrows, I
become my father's son again and argue the toss with anyone
who cares to step on my corns. And I must confess that I get a
certain manly satisfaction from the fact that I can hold my own
with the so-called big drinkers and small time gamblers of the
town. Oh yes, a hidden reservoir she tapped . . . But before we
all get carried away here I think I'd better point out to yeh that
I'm more a man in mournin' than a hawk in the night. Because
yeh see I know now for sure that she will not be comin' back to
me. And so I mourn. And I pine. And everytime I come up here
the sound of this lonely bell tells me that I'm goin' to live a long,
long time. The only consolation I have is that at least now I have
a story to tell.

Lights down on the belfry. We hear the sound of a bell ringing. Lights rise on the vestry where FATHER PAT, *a young priest, is reverently discarding his vestments after Mass.* DOMINIC, *the simple-minded altar boy, is busy trying to light the wick that is attached to a long pole.*

DOMINIC. Did I do it alright this mornin' after Father?

PAT. Yeah, yeh did a right job Dominic so yeh did. A right job boy.

DOMINIC. That's good. Artie 'll be glad to hear that anyway won't he? Hah? . . . Yeh made me put enough water in your wine anyway today Father. What was wrong with yeh? Did yeh have a bit of a thirst on yeh or what?

PAT. What? Yeah! Mind yeh don't burn yourself there. Here, show us.

PAT *goes across to light the wick.*

DOMINIC. Spwead some jam on my bwead said Fwed. Fwed's mother grew cwoss. Fwed's face gwew wed . . . Did yeh see auld Molly Delaney out there this mornin'? She nearly swallowed her false teeth prayin' that's all . . . I'm goin' to tell yeh one thing Father but that one 'll be jawlockin' herself one of these days so she will. The big mouth on her! I wonder what she's prayin' all the time for anyway? More information I suppose. Artie says that she'd go up your hole for news. She's queer nosey though ain't she? Hah? Yeh know I think she's tryin' to imitate one of those holy statues out there. She keeps lookin' up at it all the time. She's nearly after crackin' the face off it from lookin' up at it that much . . . I'd say yeh were dyin' for that fag Father were yeh?

PAT (*lighting up*). Yeah.

DOMINIC. Hoppin' off of it yeh are boy! There's an ashtray there Father. Behind yeh. That's it. Keep Artie happy.

DONAL *enters.*

DONAL. I'm sorry Father. I didn't know that you were still eh . . .

PAT. What? No, come in out of that, you're alright.

DONAL. What?

PAT. Come in will yeh.

DONAL. No it's alright Father, I'll hang on out in the car for her.

PAT. No yeh won't. Come in and sit down and wait for her. Sit down there. She won't be long. She's just changin' the flowers in the transept I think. Yeah. How are yeh keepin' anyway?

DONAL. Alright.

PAT. That's good. Dominic yeh might tell Angela that she's wanted in here as soon as yeh go out there will yeh.

DOMINIC. Yeah right. (*He goes.*)

PAT. I'm goin' to tell yeh one thing but we don't know ourselves here since she arrived. She keeps the place immaculate, that's all . . . Yes, immaculate! Oh now she's a credit to yeh.

DONAL. Ah yeh can't beat the auld woman's touch all the same though can yeh?

PAT. No. That's a fact alright. Yeh cannot beat it!

DOMINIC (*returning*). Hey Father I was right about that big statue after. There's a big crack down the face and one of the ears is hangin' off of it too.

PAT. What?

DOMINIC. Ah yeh believed me and all. The face of yeh Father! I caught yeh rightly there didn't I?

DOMINIC *leaves, laughing.*

DONAL. I'd say he's a bit of a character is he?

PAT. Oh stop, he's an awful case so he is. Of course Artie has him like that . . . Are yeh not workin' today, no?

DONAL. Yes I am. I'm on the auld four to twelve shift.

PAT. Any handball this weather?

DONAL. Yeah. That's where I'm goin' now. Down to the alley for a couple of practice games. There's a big game on this Friday night like yeh know.

PAT. Aye?

DONAL. Yeah. I'm playin' young Marty Murray for the club championship. The winner 'll be sent out to Toronto to represent the club out there.

PAT. Lovely. You were out there before of course Donal weren't yeh?

DONAL. Yeah I was out there twice before.

PAT. Well?

DONAL. I loved it out there Father. To tell yeh the truth if I was a younger man I'd emigrate in the mornin' so I would.

PAT. Would yeh?

DONAL. Yeah. God I would. In the mornin' boy!

ARTIE *enters.*

PAT. I was just sayin' to this fella here Artie that we don't know ourselves since Angela arrived do we?

ARTIE. What's that?

PAT. I say Angela keeps the place immaculate here.

ARTIE. Yeah. How are yeh Donal.

DONAL. How's it goin' Artie.

PAT. Oh yeh can't beat the woman's touch boy.

ARTIE. How did Dominic get on after?

PAT. Alright.

ARTIE. No calamities, no?

PAT. No, he was alright fate.

DONAL. Who's that in the mortuary, Artie?

ARTIE. Auld Eamey Boyle the tailor.

DONAL. Aye? When did he die?

ARTIE. The day before yesterday. He's gettin' buried tomorrow.

DONAL. He was supposed to be a terrible mean man wasn't he?

ARTIE. He wasn't too flaithiúlach anyway that's for sure.

DONAL. He wouldn't spend Christmas I believe. I heard they found a big wad of money stitched into the linin' of the auld suit that he was gettin' buried in yeh know.

ARTIE. So I heard.

DONAL. It was probably his Confirmation money Artie, hah?

ARTIE. It was probably his Confirmation suit too.

They laugh.

PAT. Yeh can't take it with yeh lads!

DONAL. I don't know! Your man made a fairly good stab at it anyway!

ARTIE *goes into the closet to put on his soutane.* PAT *is busy packing a bag with Communion hosts and annointing oils, etc.*

PAT. That young Marty Murray is supposed to be a fair little handballer ain't he?

DONAL. Yeah he's a promisin' young player alright.

PAT. It's hard to beat the youth all the same though ain't it? Hah?

DONAL. Yeah but I'd be a lot stronger than him though like, yeh know.

PAT. Yeah, I suppose. And cuter too of course.

DONAL. What? Yeah. Well I hope so anyway.

ANGELA *enters with a vase of withered flowers in each hand.*

PAT. Come on Angela, you're keepin' this good man waitin' here for yeh.

ANGELA. What's that? Oh I was wonderin' who was wantin' me here. You're early Donal.

PAT. He's anxious to see you Angela that's what it is.

ANGELA. No fear Father. Artie I haven't enough flowers to do the little shrine. Mrs Kehoe was supposed to leave me in some this mornin' but there's no sign of them and I've to go.

ARTIE. They're out in the porch there.

ANGELA. Oh are they? I never saw them.

ARTIE. They wringin' wet mind yeh.

ANGELA *dumps the withered flowers and washes the vases.*

PAT. Where have all the flowers gone hah?

ANGELA. Are yeh off Father?

PAT. Yeah. I've to go and do me rounds. Artie, I'm wantin' to call in and see your mother this mornin'. Will the key be in the door or what?

ARTIE. Yeah, more than likely. But sure auld Molly Delaney 'll probably be there with her now anyway.

PAT. Right. I'll see yez.

ARTIE. All the best.

PAT. Good luck with the game.

DONAL. Thanks very much Father.

PAT. I'll see yeh, Angela.

ANGELA. Goodbye Father.

PAT *exits.*

DONAL. Hurry up Angela will yeh.

ANGELA. Hold your horses there now Donal until I finish this.

DONAL. It's just that I'm wantin' to get down to the alley before anyone else takes it.

ANGELA. Oh now I don't think you'll be killed in the rush at this hour of the mornin' or anythin'.

DONAL. Yeh never know . . . Your man is a nice enough fella ain't he?

ANGELA. Who's that? Oh Father Pat. Ah yeah. Father Pat's a very nice man alright.

DONAL. Is he off the gargle now, yeah?

ANGELA *throws him a dirty look. Silence.*

ANGELA. When is that weddin' on Artie?

ARTIE. Tomorrow afternoon. Four o'clock.

ANGELA. Tch, we'll have a rake of confetti now all over the place.

ARTIE. Mmn. We'll have your man's funeral to contend with first of course.

ANGELA (*going out to the porch*). Oh that's right. I forgot about that.

DONAL. Yeh can't take it with yeh says Father Pat. Auld Boyle did his best to though Artie didn't he? Hah?

ARTIE. Yeah.

DONAL. Angela.

ANGELA (*off*). What?

DONAL. I say the auld tailor had a load of money stitched into the linin' of his suit, yeh know.

ANGELA (*off*). Yeah?

DONAL *laughs*.

DONAL. Cute as a fox boy . . . I'd say there's always somethin' to be done around here Artie is there?

ARTIE. Yeh'd be kept goin' alright.

DONAL. Surprisin' ain't it?

ANGELA *returns with the flowers*.

Well just as long as yeh keep this one busy while I'm out in Toronto I don't mind. Yeh won't know me when I come back hon. I'll have one of those big plaid jackets on me and a great Canadian accent and all. None of yez'll know me boy! (*He laughs.*) Were yeh ever out there Artie? No. Jaysus it's a brilliant place. I'm not coddin' yeh. Lashin's of money out there too. Sure most of their players are professional like yeh know. Not like here. We're only in the ha'penny place here. I'm goin' to tell yeh one thing but if I was a younger man . . .

ANGELA. Why, what would yeh do Donal?

DONAL. What?

ANGELA. What would yeh do if you were a younger man?

DONAL. Well I wouldn't be clockin' in on the four to twelve shift in that auld factory anyway that's for starters.

ANGELA *throws him a dirty look*.

I wouldn't Angela.

ANGELA. Oh now I think yeh fulfilled your destiny Donal, somehow or other!

DONAL. What? . . . Ain't that awful Artie? . . . Listen I'll go and bring the car around, hon. I'll meet yeh at the steps. Don't be too long now will yeh? I'll see yeh Artie.

He leaves.

ARTIE. All the best . . . Sure you go ahead if yeh want Angela. I'll finish off that for yeh.

ANGELA. Ah I'm nearly done now Artie. Will you just ask Dominic to bring them out for me?

ARTIE. Yeah.

ANGELA. These are for the shrine now.

ARTIE. Right.

ANGELA. The altar looks lovely now Artie don't it?

ARTIE. Mmn . . .

ANGELA. It do though don't it? I'm kind of proud of that now! Dominic is after missin' a few candles out there too Artie.

ARTIE. Is he? Ah I'll get them meself after.

ANGELA. Sure God help him, he tries his best don't he? You've got a hole in your soutane Artie. (*She touches the garment.* ARTIE *basks in the nearness of her.*) Oh it's Dominic's birthday tomorrow ain't it? Were you sayin' somethin' about throwin' a bit of a do for him or somethin'?

ARTIE. Yeah. Above in the belfry. Nothin' elaborate now. A bit of an auld cake and that. Just to spur him on a bit like yeh know.

ANGELA. Ah yeah.

DOMINIC (*entering*). Them flowers smell lovely out there Angela.

ANGELA. Do they hon?

DOMINIC. Things went well here this mornin' after Artie you'll be glad to know.

ARTIE. So I heard.

DOMINIC. No calamities anyway. Although auld Molly Delaney nearly swallowed her false teeth again prayin' for more information. The same one'd go up your hole for news Angela I'm not coddin' yeh. Wouldn't she Artie?

ANGELA (*fetching her coat*). Oh Dominic you're an awful case so yeh are.

DOMINIC. Yeh missed it here yesterday Angela.

ANGELA. How's that?

DOMINIC. We had a christenin' here. Twins.

ANGELA. Aw!

DOMINIC. The pair of them kicked up an awful racket here so they did. A boy and a girl. The roars of her, says Artie, and the bawls of him.

ANGELA. I'll see yeh in the mornin' Artie.

ARTIE. Goodbye Angela.

ANGELA *leaves.*

DOMINIC. Can I go up and ring the bells today Artie?

ARTIE. If yeh want.

DOMINIC. Did yeh hear me yesterday?

ARTIE. Yeah, yeh played the same hymn twice. 'Hail, Queen of Heaven'.

DOMINIC. Did I? I have a new one today. (*He sings.*) I can't get no satisfaction . . .

ARTIE. You do boy! Listen, take off that soutane in case yeh trip goin' up the stairs will yeh. And bring them flowers out to the shrine too on your way.

DOMINIC. Yeah, right . . . Did yeh ever see your man playin' handball Artie?

ARTIE. Who's that?

DOMINIC. Angela's husband. He's queer good boy. Not as good as me though. (*He mimes a handball game.*) Butt! I'll tell yeh one thing Artie, you're alright.

DOMINIC *goes into the closet to hang up his soutane.*

ARTIE. I'll be wantin' you here tomorrow afternoon for that funeral boy, do yeh hear me.

DOMINIC (*off*). I won't be able Artie.

ARTIE. Why not?

DOMINIC. I just won't, so don't keep askin' me all the time.

ARTIE *sniggers.* DOMINIC *returns with a glove in his hand.*

Angela is after forgettin' her glove Artie, look. Will I run after her with it?

ARTIE. What? No, it's alright. Give it here. She'll be gone off in the car by now anyway. Go ahead up to the belfry.

DOMINIC. Alright.

ARTIE. Here, don't forget the flowers.

DOMINIC. Leave it to me Artie. I'll make a mess of it. (*He sings.*) I can't get no satisfaction . . .

DOMINIC *leaves.* ARTIE *gazes down at the glove in his hand. Lights*

down. Lights rise on the belfry. It is the aftermath of the party.
ANGELA is sweeping the place clean. ARTIE enters.

ANGELA. That went off alright after Artie didn't it?

ARTIE. Grand.

ANGELA. I'd say he enjoyed himself anyway would you?

ARTIE. Who, Dominic? Oh yes he did. He had a right time. Sure did yeh not see the state of him? He had more cake on his face now than he ate I'd say.

ANGELA. Is that your big bowl there Artie, yeah?

ARTIE. What? Yeah.

ANGELA. I left the rest of your stuff down below in the vestry beside the sink.

ARTIE. Oh yeah right. You'd better not let me go home without anythin' anyway or there'll be war. Me Ma may be confined to bed but she still rules the roost in that kitchen. I think she has auld Molly Delaney doin' an inventory for her every week, yeh know!

ANGELA chuckles.

ANGELA. This is a great lookin' place Artie ain't it? I was never up here before today yeh know. It's queer high up ain't it. I nearly got dizzy when I looked down at the chapel that time. (*She goes and touches the rope.*) How is your mother keepin' anyway Artie?

ARTIE. Alright I suppose. Go ahead if yeh want.

ANGELA. What?

ARTIE. Go ahead. (*He urges her to ring the bell.*)

ANGELA. Yeah?

ARTIE. Yeah! (ANGELA *pulls the rope,* ARTIE *urging her on. He rises and goes to her.*). To tell yeh the truth I'm a bit worried about her – stuck up in that auld bed all the time. Although she's due to go in and have her operation shortly. The sooner the better I think! . . . Little did poor auld Boyle the tailor realise that the day would come when a woman would be ringin' his funeral bell.

ANGELA. It was probably the nearest he ever got to a woman in his life.

Slight pause.

ARTIE. It was a small enough funeral.

ANGELA. Yeah well it was a small enough life too, Artie wasn't it? There's a real lonely sound off of that ain't there? (*She rambles, reads the graffiti etc.*) The Dumper McGrath was here hah! . . . What are these?

ARTIE. The chimes. We play the hymns on them.

ANGELA. Oh right. What is it, each number represents a note or somethin' is it?

ARTIE. Yeah. There's a couple of hymns there in front of yeh. I wrote them out one time for Dominic.

ANGELA. Oh yeah. 'Hail Queen of Heaven'. 'Faith of Our Fathers'. 'Sweet Sacrament Divine'. And what's that one?

ARTIE. I don't know what that is. 'I Can't Get No Satisfaction' I think. The little divil is after figurin' it out himself. It won't be long now either! . . . But sure go ahead and play one of them if yeh want. Go on, I'll call out the numbers to yeh.

ANGELA. What? Alright . . . 'Hail Queen of Heaven'!

ARTIE. Right. Are yeh ready?

ANGELA. Yeah. No, hang on though. (*Rolls up her sleeves.*) Go on now.

ARTIE. Are yeh sure now?

ANGELA. Yeah. Fire away. Not too fast now or anythin'.

ARTIE. O.K. Five Five, Three five five. Eight eight, seven six five. Five four three two three four, three five three two. Five five, three five five.

ANGELA. We claim thy care. It's alright I have it now. Save us from peril and from woe. Mother of Christ. Star of the sea. Pray for the wanderer. Pray for me. Pray for the wanderer. Pray for me . . . That was alright wasn't it?

ARTIE. Great. Six dongs on the big bell now.

ANGELA. What? Do I? Oh right, hang on . .

ANGELA *darts across to the rope.*

Is this supposed to be joyous or sad?

ARTIE. What do yeh mean?

ANGELA. Well is it for the weddin' or the wake?

ARTIE. The weddin'.

ANGELA. Joyous!

She rings the bell. ARTIE *watches her.*

Why do yeh think people need to hear the sound of bells Artie?

ARTIE. I don't know. I've never been married and I'm not dead yet so I wouldn't know . . . It's supposed to make us all feel equal or somethin' ain't it? I don't know. It don't make me feel equal anyway.

ANGELA. It's the only time I ever feel really at home here yeh know – when I hear the bells ringin'. Funny ain't it? . . . What do yeh mean, you don't feel equal?

ARTIE. What? Ah I don't know. I'm not bankin' on a large funeral Angela, let's put it that way.

ANGELA. How do yeh mean?

ARTIE. Sometimes my life feels kind of small too yeh know.

ANGELA. Yeah but your life is not over though Artie is it?

Silence. ARTIE *looks at her. She stares into his eyes. She goes to him. He takes her in his arms. They kiss. Lights down. Lights rise on the vestry where* FATHER PAT *is putting on his coat.* ARTIE *enters.*

ARTIE (*to the audience*). A man's life can change on him overnight yeh know. It does a little somersault and he wakes up one morning to find himself on the far side of a river that he never meant to cross. It might be a bit of a fall that he gets. He'll break a leg or chip a bone maybe. Or it might be a few auld hasty words that he says to someone in the heat of the moment one day. Whatever it is he soon realises that things will never be the same again and he learns the meaning of the word 'destiny'. For me it was that kiss. It was like a trap door that I stepped on and fell through and before I knew it I was goin' around the place like a man possessed, wonderin' where she was all the time and what she was up to. I'm not coddin' yeh I used to think my workin' day would never be done so that I could shut up shop and go up into the belfry and wait for her to come to me. Another man's wife!

ARTIE *hangs his head.* FATHER PAT *makes to leave.*

ARTIE. If you're goin' out through the chapel Father yeh might tell Molly Delaney that I'm wantin' to lock up now, will yeh.

PAT. Yeah right Artie.

FATHER PAT *leaves. Lights down. Lights rise on the belfry. The contents of the basket are spilled out onto the ground – garments and curtains and cushions etc.* ARTIE *and* ANGELA *are sprawled out on them, their backs to the basket, snuggling into one another.* ARTIE *has a photograph in his hand.*

ARTIE. She knows well enough what I'm up to I think. She can hear me climbin' up into the attic and rootin' around in the auld biscuit tins and all. 'Come down out of there Artie O'Leary. You'll fall!'

ANGELA. Ah God help her.

ARTIE. They were never married yeh know. I checked back through the books in the vestry and there's no record of them ever gettin' married. I found nothin' above in the attic either.

ANGELA. So what do yeh think happened then?

ARTIE. I don't know. I suppose she got pregnant and me Grand Da who was the sacristan here at the time probably objected to them gettin' married or somethin'. I mean to say by all accounts me Da was a bit of a Jack the Lad from what I can gather.

ANGELA. And is that when he went away?

ARTIE. No, he didn't go away for a few years as far as I know. I was about three I think. Two and a half maybe.

ANGELA. You don't remember him though?

ARTIE. No . . . I have a kind of vague recollection of a man standin' over me one day, a suitcase at his feet. The sun was shinin' in my eyes. It must have been the summer. When he bent down to say hello to me I started to cry and he sang a little song to try and shut me up. (*He sings.*) 'Tell her that I'm blue and lonely. Dreaming Carolina Moon . . . ' I don't know if it was him or not to tell yeh the truth. It's kind of hard for me to separate the things I remember about him from all the things I've heard down through the years like yeh know. And then of course I wasn't allowed to ask any questions about him either. I mean to say yeh couldn't even mention his name without drivin' me mother into a litany of abuse about him so . . . All I knew about him was that he was real tall. And lean. And he wore a hat all the time. And a woman once told me he had a deadly smile.

ANGELA. He looks like an interestin' man. I bet he was good with women. Like you!

ARTIE. Like me! You must be jokin'!

ANGELA. Hah?

She touches his face and smiles. They kiss.

ARTIE. You're really lovely, do yeh know that? Your face! I was watchin' yeh the other day as you were dressin' and the sun was shinin' on your face and I'm not coddin' yeh, I couldn't take my eyes off of you.

ANGELA. I know. I saw yeh lookin' at me.

ARTIE. Did yeh?

ANGELA (*kissing him*). Mmn . . .

ARTIE. I just can't stop thinkin' about you Angela. All the time! I can't seem to get yeh out of my head. All day long. I see yeh walkin' away from me or comin' towards me. I see your little bike in the porch, your scarf draped across a chair, your coat hangin' up in the closet, maybe your gloves lyin' around. And then I'll hear yeh whisperin' to some auld one out in the chapel and the sound of your voice makes me want to run to yeh. I want to kiss away everything that ever happened to yeh so that there's no one and nothin' left but you and me. Just the two of us. Wouldn't that be nice? No one and nothin' but the two of us hah?

ANGELA. Do yeh know somethin' Artie O'Leary, one of these days I'm goin' to just melt in your arms yeh know – listenin' to yeh. There'll be nothin' left only my shadow on the wall and then where will yeh be, hah?

ARTIE. I don't know. Tell me. Where will I be? . . .

They kiss. Pause.

ANGELA. I went up to see my sister Maude this afternoon . . . I wanted to tell her all about yeh. But I couldn't. It's funny, there was a time when we used to tell each other everythin'. Until I discovered that I was doin' all the talkin'. We used to go nearly everywhere together – myself and Maude – off to all the dances and all. We were as mad as hatters, the pair of us. Well I was anyway! (*She chuckles.*)

ARTIE. What?

ANGELA. We joined the Irish dancin' one time. We used to come out onto the back of an auld lorry or somewhere and your man'd start up on the accordion. Bum bum bum bum bum bum bum. Bum bum bum bum bum bum bum . . . All the boys'd gather round and try to look up our dresses. Meself and Maude used to give them a right eye full I can tell yeh.

ARTIE. Were yeh any good?

ANGELA. At what? Dancin'? No we weren't. Sure we hardly ever practised or anythin'. I just wanted to get up and show off in front of the crowd like yeh know. I probably should have been a singer in a band or somethin' Artie shouldn't I? When we were young I was forever draggin' poor Maude down to stand outside the Town Hall every Friday night. It was durin' the Rock 'N Roll days and we could see them all jivin' inside – the boys in their snazzy suits, the girls in their big dresses and all. I used to be dyin' to go in there. I'd've loved that now – clackin' along in me high heel shoes . . . By the time we were old enough to go though the whole scene had started to change . . . Keep away from Padraic Lacy, me mother said to me when we were goin' off to our very first dance. Why? says I. Never mind why, says she. Just keep away from him that's all. Padraic Lacy had a car and there was a rumour goin' around that he had slipped a girl a Mickey Finn one night after a dance and while she was drowsy he put his hand up her skirt. He was one of the first boys I ever went out with. I thought he was a right creep. He started to cry when I told him I didn't want to see him again. Maude was lookin' for a prince or some sort of a sheik to whisk her off to God knows where. She was goin' out with this fella from Tuam who came to town to work in the bank. A real good lookin' fella with sultry eyes. Maude dropped him like a hot brick when she found out that his Da was a plasterer. She was a real snob. She married a guard in the end and went off to live in suburbia . . . I never really wanted all the things that other people seem to long for Artie yeh know. Maybe that's why I got them hah? . . . Donal is still down in the dumps over that auld handball match. The young fella ran rings around him I heard. He won't go out nor nothin' now. He just mopes around the house all day drinkin' mugs of tay. I think he feels it's an end of an era or somethin'. And maybe he's right . . .

She looks into ARTIE's *worried eyes. She takes his hand.*

ARTIE. What are we goin' to do Angela?

ANGELA. I don't know.

ARTIE. We could go away together somewhere. I could get a job.

ANGELA. I can't go away Artie. What about Donal and the children. I mean to say I can't just up and go like . . . (*A noise off.*) What's that?

ARTIE. What?

ANGELA. There's somebody up there, Artie.

They rise and rustle about for their shoes, etc.

ANGELA. Did yeh see my coat anywhere Artie?

ARTIE. What?

The tower door opens.

DOMINIC (*emerging*). Artie!

ARTIE. Dominic! What are you doin' here at this hour of the night?

ANGELA. Dominic were you spyin' on us?

DOMINIC. What? No!

ARTIE. What's up Dominic?

DOMINIC. Me Uncle is after puttin' me out of the house, Artie.

ARTIE. When?

DOMINIC. A couple of days ago.

ARTIE. What for?

DOMINIC. I don't know.

ARTIE. Now Dominic, yeh do know.

DOMINIC. He said that he was goin' to send me to a special school Artie, so I ran away.

ARTIE. Did he put yeh out now or did yeh run away, which?

DOMINIC. I ran away. He said that he was goin' send me to this special school Artie and I might not like the food there. I only ates chips yeh know.

ARTIE. Where do your Uncle think yeh are now?

DOMINIC. I don't know. With you I think.

ARTIE. You told him that you were stoppin' with me did yeh?

DOMINIC. Yeah. (*He weeps.*)

ARTIE. So you've been sleepin' here have yeh?

DOMINIC *nods.*

ANGELA (*fetching her coat and things*). Listen Artie, I'm goin' to go. You make sure that he don't say nothin' to no one about seein' us here together won't yeh?

ARTIE. What? Yeah.

ANGELA. It gives me the creeps anyone sneakin' up on me like that. How did he get in here anyway?

ARTIE. He has a spare key to the belfry . . . He meant no harm Angela.

Pause ANGELA *goes to the boy.*

ANGELA. Don't cry now Dominic. Here dry your eyes now like a good boy and don't cry. Sure Artie'll look after yeh, won't yeh Artie?

ARTIE. Yeah.

ANGELA. Now. Good boy Dominic . . . I'll go Artie.

ARTIE. What? Oh hang on and I'll let yeh out.

ARTIE *and* ANGELA *leave. Pause.* ARTIE *returns.*

DOMINIC. What am I'm goin' to do Artie?

ARTIE. I don't know. Yeh can't stay here anyway that's for sure. It's a wonder yeh didn't get your death. Where did yeh sleep anyway?

DOMINIC. The basket!

ARTIE (*stuffing all the garments, etc. back into the basket*). You may come home with me for a few nights. I'll go up and see your Uncle tomorrow or the next day just to see what he wants to do about yeh.

DOMINIC. Alright. Another calamity Artie.

ARTIE. Yeah. But sure what harm, we'll manage.

DOMINIC. I'm a royal headache though ain't I?

ARTIE. Yeh are boy! King Coitus Interruptus the Second.

DOMINIC *splutters out a laugh through his tears.*

Listen Dominic, I don't want you to say anythin' to anyone about seein' meself and Angela here together do yeh hear me? It's a kind of secret like, yeh know.

DOMINIC. What? Alright Artie, I won't say nothin to no one about it, honest.

ARTIE. Good lad. Come on now . . .

Lights down. Lights rise on the vestry. ARTIE *and* DOMINIC *are sitting at the table which is littered with cardboard boxes and old biscuit tins full of documents and photographs, etc.* DOMINIC *is listening to a walkman as he rummages.*

DOMINIC. There's one of you Artie! Who's that on your shoulders eh? (*A photograph.*)

ARTIE (*engrossed in a letter*). What?

DOMINIC. Who's the child on your shoulders?

ARTIE. Show us?

DOMINIC. Where was that taken Artie? The Katts Strand is it?

ARTIE. That's me on his shoulders be Jaysus. Yeh know I think I remember that day. He carried me on his shoulders along a beach. We stopped at an auld dilapidated boat that was all covered in seaweed and all. He had a blue shirt on him – like the sky . . . I remember . . . Or do I?

DOMINIC. That's the Katts Strand Artie. That's where that boat is anyway . . .

ARTIE. What?

DOMINIC. I have no photographs at home at all. Me Aunty burnt them all on me.

ARTIE. Why did she do that?

DOMINIC. I don't know. She said it'd be better to get rid of them . . Yeh see Artie what you don't understand is that me Aunty is really me Mammy yeh see.

ARTIE. Well she's certainly like a Mammy to yeh anyway Dominic ain't she?

DOMINIC. No she is me Mammy really – me real Mammy. The only thing is me Uncle don't know that.

ARTIE. Oh!

DOMINIC. You're not to say that to no one now Artie. Me Uncle don't know nothin' about that yeh know.

FATHER PAT *enters.*

PAT. Well, are yeh hard at it?

ARTIE. How are yeh Pat.

DOMINIC. I'm goin' to tell yeh one thing Father but there's a fella in one of those pictures there and he must be Artie's Da because he's the spittin' image of him boy! Show it to him there Artie.

ARTIE. What? . . . Were yeh over in the house Pat?

PAT. Yeah.

ARTIE. Is me mother alright?

PAT. Yeah, she's alright. Molly Delaney was makin' her a cup of tea as I was comin' out there.

DOMINIC. Well rather her than me then Father because there's no pleasin' that woman, boy. I brought her up a cup of tea this mornin' and she told me it wasn't near sweet enough. I wouldn't mind but I had put loads of sugar into it. I brought it back down and I put a heap more in it. I'd say she thought it was a toffee apple she was atin' it was that sweet . . . I'd say that's the Katts Strand in that picture alright though Artie would you?

ARTIE. Yeah.

PAT (*thumbing through a newspaper*). I see young Marty Murray is on his way to Toronto anyway Artie.

ARTIE. So I see.

PAT. He's a great future in front of him that young lad has. Sure I believe he horsed Donal in the final.

ARTIE. Yeah. So I heard.

DOMINIC. Oh that reminds me Father you left your Polo mints here this mornin' after yeh. And yeh needn't go blamin' me for atin' them on yeh either. I only ate one or two of them. Angela took the rest.

ARTIE. Why, was Angela here this mornin' Dominic?

DOMINIC. Yeah. She was lookin' for you, Artie.

ARTIE. Was she? What time was this at now?

DOMINIC. I don't know. (*He sings along with the music.*) 'Don't play with me 'cause you're playin' with fire . . .'

PAT. I haven't seen Angela for a couple of days. Was she sick or anythin' I wonder?

ARTIE. I don't know.

PAT. By the way your mother's not exactly over the moon about you-know-who stayin' in the house either Artie yeh know.

ARTIE. Yeah I know. But sure it'll be only for a couple of more days. Just until I can get him settled in the school.

PAT. Yeah well she's a bit worried about you too, I don't mind tellin' yeh.

ARTIE. How do you mean?

PAT. She says you're stayin' out 'til all hours of the night lately. She hinted that she asked Molly Delaney to keep an eye on yeh but yeh keep givin' her the slip all the time. She thinks you're after takin' to the drink. You're not are yeh?

ARTIE throws him a dirty look. Slight pause.

ARTIE. What's wrong with yeh?

PAT. Ah I don't know. I'm addled. I mean you'd think you'd be bad. I went in to see this auld fella this mornin'. Yeh should have seen him Artie. His face was as gaunt. His eyes sunk back in his head. Do yeh know what he was like now. He was like a man with no soul inside of him, that's what he was like. Not long for this world either I'd say. And what a story! He lost two children when he was a young man he was tellin' me. He lost his wife, he lost his job, he lost his health and in the end he lost his faith. And who could blame the man. And I'm supposed to minister to him. I'm supposed to tell him what he doesn't know, what he hasn't figured out already himself. I don't know . . . (*He shakes his head and sighs.*)

ARTIE. Just sit and listen to him Pat if I was you. That's probably all he wants anyway – someone to talk to.

PAT. Yeah . . . Fancy tradin' places with me Artie no?

ARTIE *shakes his head and chuckles.*

DOMINIC. Did yeh show him the snap of your Da yet Artie?

ARTIE. No.

DOMINIC. Why not? You're very down lookin' Father ain't yeh?
What's wrong with yeh?

PAT. I'm surrounded by the dead and the dyin' Dominic that's
what's wrong with me. Yes, the dead and the dyin', boy!

DOMINIC. All the more reason to cheer up a bit ain't it. I mean to
say it could be worse. It could be you! (*He laughs.*) Look at me.
I'm always in good form. Ain't I Artie?

DOMINIC *goes back to the music.*

PAT (*chuckling*). We're goin' to have to do somethin' about him
Artie. Put him on a stage or somethin'!

Pause. Lights down. Lights rise. In the background FATHER PAT
and ANGELA *are preparing for the party in the belfry.* ARTIE *is
standing downstage, facing the audience.*

ARTIE (*to the audience*). My father was carryin' me on his shoulders
along a beach, to a place where I'd never been before, to a place
where I'm sure I'd long to stay and his shirt was the colour of
the sky. I probably smelt the sea and heard the sea gulls cry.
And then he brought me home again . . . Is that what I was tryin'
to do for Dominic when I brought him to live with me – carry
him on my shoulders to a place where he'd never been before? Is
that why I organised the party for him? Who knows? Deep and
meaningless questions hah! Yeh know whenever I remember that
party I don't think of Dominic at all now. It's meself and Angela
that I see. In fact sometimes I have to wonder who was carryin'
who!

PAT. God it's amazin' what a few flowers can do about the place
too ain't it Angela? Hah?

ANGELA. Yeah, they brighten up the place a bit alright don't
they. Do yeh think it's alright now?

PAT. Yeah, it's lovely. Fair play to yeh. It's a credit to yeh so it
is . . He'll get some land when he comes up here though won't
he? God help him.

ANGELA. Yeah, he surely will!

ARTIE *enters.*

ARTIE. You two know what to do now don't yeh?

PAT. God we do, don't we Angela? Leave it to us Artie, we'll make a mess of it.

ARTIE. Right. Where's the cake Angela?

ANGELA. It's inside there on the ground.

ARTIE. Good. Right, I'll go down and get him. You two make sure that yeh duck out of sight.

ARTIE *takes one last look around, smiles at* ANGELA *and leaves.*

ANGELA. I think Artie is more excited about this than Dominic's goin' to be.

PAT. More than likely. All the lads are dyin' about Artie though Angela yeh know. When I was an altar boy here Artie was the one we'd all turn to if we were in any sort of trouble. He was only after takin' over as sacristan here that time. Sure I suppose he wasn't much more than a chap himself when I think of it. But he used to bring us all up into the belfry to watch him ringin' the bells. I used to be terrified lookin' at him swingin' out of the rope. I'm not coddin' yeh he was as wild as a March hare now the same fella. The hunchback from Notre Dame had nothin' on him boy. We'd all go down underneath the church then – The Catacombs Artie used to call it. He built us a little sort of a club down there and all. One of the lads knocked off a bottle of altar wine one time and we all got drunk down there. We were all as sick as pigs after it. Artie came down and caught us. There was war boy . . . He never said anythin' about it though, fair play to him. He never hung us! . . . Poor auld Artie – the salt of the earth boy!

ANGELA. So this is the only life he's ever known then, really?

PAT. Oh yeah. The only life any of us has ever known if the truth be told . . Yes! . . . I'd think we'd better vamoose Angela before we're caught red-handed here.

ANGELA. Yeah. I don't know what's keepin' Donal with the present. I wouldn't mind but I told him to be here on time.

PAT. Oh don't yeh know where he is Angela – down in the handball alley. Seventh Heaven for him. Come on in the name of God.

PAT *goes into the shadows.* ANGELA *takes a last good look around and then she does likewise. Pause.* ARTIE *and* DOMINIC *enter.*

DOMINIC. Hey Artie, what's goin' on here?

ARTIE. What?

DOMINIC. Look at the state of the place.

ARTIE. Oh yeah! That's queer ain't it?

Suddenly ANGELA *and* PAT *emerge from the shadows, party hats on their heads with blowers and streamers etc.*

ANGELA. Happy Birthday Dominic.

PAT. Happy birthday me auld son.

DOMINIC. What? Oh be Jaysus look at the queer one where she is Artie. And look at the head on your man! Hah?

ARTIE (*taking a few parcelled presents from his pockets*). Happy Birthday Dominic.

ANGELA (*kissing him*). Happy Birthday Dominic.

DOMINIC. Whawhoo, did yeh see that Artie.

PAT (*giving him a present*). Here y'are Dominic, see what yeh make of that.

DOMINIC. More presents! It's well for me Artie ain't it?

ARTIE. Well it is your birthday. Pour out the drinks there Angela will yeh. Are yeh wantin' some trifle Dominic?

DOMINIC. Yes please.

ANGELA. What are you drinkin' Father?

PAT. I'll have an orange juice Angela please.

ANGELA. Artie?

ARTIE. I'll have a bottle of stout Angela. Are you wantin' some of this trifle Father?

PAT. Aye, why not!

ARTIE. There y'are Dominic, get that into yeh. Oh by the way I see auld Molly Delaney down in the chapel prayin' Dominic, do yeh want me to ask her up or what?

DOMINIC. Leave her where she is Artie. We don't want that one dribblin' all over us. Sure she'd ate all the grub in one gobble boy.

DONAL (*rapping on the door*). Anybody home?

ARTIE. Here's Donal. Come in Donal.

ANGELA. Here he is now. It's about time. What kept yeh?

DONAL. I was lookin' all over the place for this thing. (*The present.*) You told me it was on the mantelpiece. On the bed it was all the time.

ANGELA. Give it here to me.

DONAL. How are yeh Father?

PAT. Hello Donal, how are yeh keepin'?

DONAL. Alright.

ANGELA. He's late again Father that's what he is. As usual! Probably paradin' around that auld stupid handball alley I suppose.

DONAL. Ain't that awful Father, what I've to put up with.

PAT. Hey, don't you say a word about our Angela or you'll have me and Artie to contend with. Ain't that right Artie? You should be kissin' the ground she walks on boy.

DONAL. Kiss the ground she walks on! Father I worship it. Sure why wouldn't I? It's costin' me forty-five quid a week just to live on it. (*He laughs.*) Ah I'm only jokin' yeh, hon.

ANGELA. Here y'are Dominic. Happy Birthday hon.

DOMINIC. Thanks very much Angela.

DONAL. Happy Birthday son.

ARTIE. What are you drinkin' Donal?

DONAL. What? I'll have a bottle of stout Artie.

ARTIE. Right.

PAT. I thought you were supposed to be in trainin' boy?

DONAL. Medicinal Father.

ARTIE. Now Donal.

DONAL. Thanks Artie.

ARTIE. Has everybody got a drink now? Yeah? Dominic, where's your drink?

ANGELA. There it is on the basket Dominic look.

ARTIE. Right, a toast to Dominic. To Dominic!

ALL (*toasting*). To Dominic.

PAT. God bless yeh.

DOMINIC. Youse are all mad.

ARTIE *winks at* ANGELA *and then he slips away into the shadows.*
FATHER PAT *and* DONAL *converse while* DOMINIC *continues
opening his presents.*

ANGELA. Are yeh alright Dominic? Can yeh manage?

DOMINIC. Yeah. Look what Artie gave me Angela. (*A walkman.*)

ANGELA. That's lovely Dominic. Do yeh know how to work it and
all yeah?

DOMINIC. Yeah. That's simple. The Dumper McGrath has one
the very axe same as this. He thinks he's a great fella.

DOMINIC *rigs it up and seeing a tape inside proceeds to listen to it, a
gleeful smile on his face as he does so.*

ANGELA. Is there a good sound off of it?

DOMINIC. Yeah. Brilliant boy! (*He sings.*) 'I Can't Get No
Satisfaction . . .'

ANGELA *chuckles. She turns to* DONAL.

ANGELA. The shouts of him.

DONAL. What tape did he get?

ANGELA. The Best of the Rolling Stones.

DONAL. That's a bit before his time ain't it. (*He sings and mimes.*)
'I'm just a little red rooster da da da dado . . .'

ARTIE *emerges from the shadows with the birthday cake, a big candle
stuck in the centre of it.*

ARTIE (*sings*). Happy Birthday to You
Happy Birthday to You (*The others join in.*)
Happy Birthday dear Dominic
Happy Birthday to you.

ANGELA. Ah Artie where did yeh get the big candle?

ARTIE. Come on now Dominic, yeh have to blow out this candle
from at least six feet back.

DOMINIC. What?

ARTIE (*putting the cake down on the basket*). Stand back there Dominic. Come on.

DOMINIC *tries in vain to blow out the candle.*

ANGELA. Ah Artie!

ARTIE (*producing a long extinguishing pole from the chapel*). Here y'are Dominic, is this any use to yeh.

They all laugh. DOMINIC *takes the pole and puts out the candle. They all cheer and then they all sing 'For He's a Jolly Good Fellow'.*

ANGELA. Give us an auld song now Dominic on this day of days.

DOMINIC. What?

ARTIE. Yeah go on Dominic. Sing us a song. Come on now. (*He sings.*) I can't get no satisfaction. I can't get no . . .

ANGELA. He's thirsty.

DOMINIC *is lowering a glass of lemonade.*

ARTIE. The big swallow on him.

DONAL. He'll be a fair man to drop pints in a few years won't he?

ANGELA. He's not goin' to drink when he grows up he was tellin' me. Sure you're not Dominic?

DOMINIC. No. I promised me Aunty.

PAT. That's right Dominic, you must always keep your promise.

ANGELA. Go on anyway Dominic and sing us the song.

DOMINIC. I will in me hat?

ANGELA. Go on out of that.

DOMINIC. But sure the only song I know is 'I Peeped in', and that's borin'.

ANGELA. 'I Peeped In'! What's that?

ARTIE. 'Scarlet Ribbons'!

ANGELA. Scarlet Ribbons. Sure that's a lovely song Dominic. Go ahead and sing that one.

DOMINIC. It's too long Angela. We'd be here all day woman . . . I'll sing a different one. No, I'll say a poem though.

ANGELA. Alright, say a poem.

DOMINIC. Matthew, Mark, Luke and John.
  Went to bed with nothin' on
  One said right
  One said shite
  And one said fuck it sure we'll stay the night . . .

ANGELA. Does that child ever think of anythin' else.

ARTIE. Eat your trifle there Dominic. Are yeh wantin' some ice
  cream on it?

DOMINIC. Yes please.

ARTIE. Give him another drop of lemonade there too Angela will
  yeh.

DOMINIC. Spwead some jam on my bwead said Fwed. I have a
  noble call now and I call on Artie to sing a song.

ARTIE. What?

PAT. Yeah, go on Artie, give us an auld blast there.

DONAL. Go on Artie.

ARTIE. Ah!

DOMINIC. Sing 'Carolina Moon', Artie. Did yeh ever hear him
  singin' that one Angela? He's always singin' that boy. I loves it.

ANGELA. Go ahead Artie.

ARTIE. Well you have to all join in with me.

DONAL. Oh we'll give yeh an auld hand there, go on out of that.

ARTIE. Alright. (*He sings.*) Carolina Moon, keep shining,
  Shining on the one who waits for me . . .

  The others join in.

  (*Song:*) Carolina Moon I'm pining
  Pining for the place I long to be
  How I'm hoping tonight you'll go
  Go to the right window
  Carry your light
  Say I'm alright
  Please do . . .

During the song ARTIE *has opened another bottle of stout for* DONAL *and refilled everyone's glass.*

ARTIE. Do yeh know somethin' Angela, but you really know how to brighten up a place alright don't yeh?

ANGELA. What? Ah yeah, a few auld flowers make all the difference alright don't they?

ARTIE. Flowers? Who said anythin' about flowers?

(*Song.*) Tell her that I'm blue and lonely
Dreaming Carolina Moon.

Lights down. Lights rise. ARTIE *is standing downstage, facing the audience. In the background* ANGELA *is humming, 'Carolina Moon' as she works in the belfry, clearing up after the party.*

ARTIE (*to the audience*). To tell yeh the truth I never heard the alarm bells ringin'. I suppose I was kind of preoccupied between one thing and another. So I never heard them ringin'. Angela hadn't turned up at the chapel for a few days. I thought it might be some sort of a little game that she was playin' with me. Of course I was pinin' inside for the sight of her but I was kind of excited too because at any moment I was half expectin' her to walk through the door. I started analysin' all the things she had said to me the last time we met and I tried to imagine what it would be like if we were really finished, knowin' in my heart and soul that we weren't finished at all of course. Baskin' in the pleasure of the pain of it all I was. Time dragged by real slow and every little thing seemed to remind me of her – the mornin', the night, a song on the radio. I kept watchin' the door of the vestry. Every knock, every rustle, every little rap and my heart'd go racin'. I tried to retrace my own footsteps to see how it had come to pass that a little spark from her heart could've set my whole world on fire. I mean I know that first time was more or less out of my control. There was nothin' I could've done about that. After that I became wary though. I pulled away for a while. I held back a little bit. I was afraid of my life that we'd get caught to tell yeh the truth. I mean I can't say that I enjoyed it or anythin'. It was too dangerous like yeh know! Although lookin' back on it all now every single minute I spent with her seemed to throw up some little jewel for me to dote on – the smell of her hair, the sound of her voice, the taste of her kiss, her laugh and the way she used to talk to me . . .

In the end I'm not coddin' yeh they were all piled up around me
– a great big tower of things – and I was runnin' towards her
with open arms, disregardin' the danger, disregardin' everything.
I'll tell yeh I just wanted her to put a lock on my heart and
throw away the key I loved her that much. I just loved her yeh
know! . . . Oh I didn't tell yeh did I? I went up to see Dominic's
Uncle after. He told me he wanted to send the boy to a special
industrial school. Dominic was becomin' a bit of a handful he
said and they couldn't really manage him all that well any more.
I suggested that maybe we could sort of ease Dominic into it. I
could borrow Father Pat's car one afternoon and drive him up
there so he could take a good look around it and that. Dominic's
Uncle thought this was a great idea. His wife just sat there. She
hardly said a word. I don't think she wanted the boy to go.
There were tears in her eyes as she led me to the door. She said
somethin' but I didn't hear her. I was miles away – thinkin' about
Angela again I was . . . No, I never heard the alarm bells ringin'.

Lights down on the belfry. Lights rise on the vestry. DOMINIC *is sitting
in a chair while* FATHER PAT *paces around the room agitated,
smoking a cigarette.*

PAT. And I suppose yeh thought that was funny did yeh? 'I Can't
   Get No Satisfaction' ringin' out all over the parish. Well I'm goin'
   to tell yeh one thing Dominic but I don't think it's funny. I'm not
   laughin' boy. And the parishioners won't think it's funny either
   and the bishop won't think it's funny. Nobody's laughin'
   Dominic, that's how funny it was.

DOMINIC. I'm sorry Father.

PAT. Oh you're sorry now are yeh? You're sorry! That's supposed
   to make everything alright is it? You're sorry. If I remember
   correctly you were sorry too when yeh climbed out onto the roof
   of the chapel last year and when yeh changed the hands of the
   clock. You were sorry when you got caught goin' up into the
   pulpit. You're sorry!

ARTIE enters.

He's sorry! Did yeh hear it?

ARTIE. Yeah.

PAT. Ringin' out all over the parish for all the world to hear.

ARTIE. I don't think anyone twigged it, Father.

PAT. Let's hope not or I'll have the bishop down on me like a ton
of bricks. I don't know. I mean to say Artie I've enough on my
plate now without this sort of thing to contend with.

ARTIE. I know.

PAT. Tch . . .

Pause.

DOMINIC. Does this mean that I won't be let ring the bells any
more Artie?

PAT. Ring the bells! You don't go next or near that belfry again
boy do yeh hear me? Stay away from it altogether. Ring the bells!
I've a good mind not to allow yeh to serve mass any more after
this. He's gettin' too big Artie anyway.

ARTIE. But sure there's no real harm done Pat is there? Like I
said I wouldn't say anyone even twigged it only ourselves.

PAT. It's alright for you Artie. I'm responsible for this place yeh
know. I'm responsible for everything here – the chapel, the
vestry, the belfry, the roof, the clock, everything. The whole
shebang falls on my shoulders and I don't need this kind of
codology I can tell yeh. I don't need it one bit. Not one little
bit . . .

ARTIE. Alright Pat, take it easy. Calm down.

PAT (*stumping out his cigarette, jittery*). I mean to say if the bishop
hears about this he'll be down on me. He won't be down on you
or Father Matthews Artie. It's me he'll be after.

ARTIE. Look Pat, why don't yeh go on over to the manse and
have a cup of tea. Go ahead.

PAT. I can't. I've confessions in a minute. You just keep that
young fella out of my way in the future. Stay out of that belfry
boy, do yeh hear me?

DOMINIC. Alright Father.

PAT. I mean it Artie. We're goin' to have a talk you and me about
him. Because I've just had it with him now. I'm up to here with
it all boy.

PAT *leaves. Pause.*

ARTIE. What am I goin' to do with you eh boy? Hah?

DOMINIC. I don't know. I'm in hot water again Artie.

ARTIE *sniggers*.

ARTIE. What did yeh think of the school after?

DOMINIC. What school?

ARTIE. You know well enough what school. What did yeh think of it?

DOMINIC. It's rotten. I hates it.

ARTIE. It's not rotten.

DOMINIC. It is rotten and I'm not goin' there.

ARTIE. Look Dominic . . .

DOMINIC. I'm not goin' there Artie so don't keep askin' me all the time.

ARTIE. That school is one of the best in the country boy.

DOMINIC. Spwead some jam on my bwead said Fwed . .

ARTIE. If you were to go to that school for a couple of years . .

DOMINIC. Fwed's mother gwew cwoss.

ARTIE. I can guarantee yeh it'll do yeh the world of good.

DOMINIC. Fwed's face gwew wed.

ARTIE. You'd get a job in next to no time so yeh would Dominic I swear.

DOMINIC. Spwead some jam on my bwead said Fwed . .

ARTIE. Listen to me Dominic, will yeh.

DOMINIC. Fwed's mother gwew cwoss.

ARTIE. Dominic, listen to me, listen to me . . .

DOMINIC. No. What if I piss in the bed? Supposin' I piss in the bed.

ARTIE. But sure Dominic the people up there are well used to all that kind of stuff boy.

DOMINIC. And supposin' they turned the light off. I don't like sleepin' with the light off. I'm afraid of the dark. I don't like the dark.

ARTIE. I'll tell them all that Dominic.

DOMINIC. They won't listen. They never listen. Somebody might tell ghost stories. I don't like anyone tellin' me ghost stories Artie and I only ates chips. I won't ate nothin' else. They'll make me ate ordinary potatoes and I only ates chips Artie.

ARTIE. Alright Dominic, you're alright. Settle down now. You're alright.

DOMINIC. I don't want to go there Artie. I don't want to go there.

ARTIE. Alright, forget about it. We'll talk about it after.

DOMINIC. I only ates chips Artie like, yeh know.

ARTIE. I know. You're alright now. Are yeh alright?

DOMINIC. What? Yeah. I'm alright Artie.

ARTIE. Good boy. I don't know what I'm goin' to do with yeh at all. What am I goin' to do with yeh eh? Hah? . . . Listen, go get your coat, I'm wantin' yeh to do a bit of a message for me.

DOMINIC. Alright . . . What are yeh wantin' me to get for yeh Artie?

ARTIE. I'm wantin' yeh to get me two hundred-watt bulbs. I need to put a bit of light on the subject here.

DOMINIC. Right. But sure as the sewin' machine said to the nudist Artie, 'Sew what?' Do yeh get it Artie? Sew what? Nothin' to sew . . . (*He laughs.*)

DONAL *enters*

DONAL. I need a baptismal cert.

ARTIE. Right . . . Is it for yourself Donal, yeah?

DONAL. Yeah.

ARTIE *opens up a big ledger.*

Quinn. February '48. Donal, Michael . . .

Pause.

ARTIE. Quinn. Donal, Michael . . How is Angela?

DONAL. She's alright.

ARTIE. I haven't seen her for a few days. She's not sick or anything is she?

DONAL. Angela's O.K.

DOMINIC *is standing in the doorway of the closet. He seems to sense the danger.* ARTIE *writes out the certificate, dries it and hands it to* DONAL. DONAL *reads it, tears it to shreds and then proceeds to scatter it like confetti over* ARTIE's *head.*

That's what you think of me isn't it? I don't really exist as far as you're concerned. Sure I'm not a Christian at all am I?

ARTIE. What do yeh mean? What are yeh talkin' about?

DONAL. Whorin' around with another man's wife that's what I mean. Playin' around like two little bats in a belfry that's what I'm talkin' about. Yeah!

ARTIE. Look Donal, I think you'd better go home and talk to Angela about this.

DONAL. I've already confronted her with it.

ARTIE. What did she say?

DONAL. She didn't need to say anything. I already knew the whole story.

ARTIE. What?

DONAL. A crooked little hand told me Artie. A crooked little hand boy! Do yeh know somethin' I ought to plaster you off of these four friggin' walls here, that's what I should do. I mean to say a man works hard, dreams hard for his wife and family only to come home one day and discover that she's whorin' around with a gobshite like you. A feckin' little mammy's boy, be Jaysus. I wouldn't mind but I gave her everythin' she ever wanted. Every inch of me went into the buildin' of that house and home. Every inch of me boy! A hundred and ten per cent. And now I find out that she's carryin' on with you behind me back. A right pair of hypocrites yeh are as far as I can see – swannin' around this place every day as if butter wouldn't melt in your mouths . . . So what am I supposed to do now then? Hah? What am I supposed to do? Of course maybe you have somethin' that I haven't got is that it? Hah? No come on, tell me. Just once I'd like someone to tell me what it is that I haven't fuckin' got . . . (DOMINIC *sniggers.*) . . . What are you laughin' at? I'll wipe that smile off of your face now very quick so I will boy.

ARTIE. Leave him out of it.

DONAL (*going for* DOMINIC). I'll break his feckin' face for him.

ARTIE (*grabbing his arm*). Leave him alone I said.

DONAL *struggles to break free from* ARTIE's *grip but* ARTIE *is too strong for him. Pause.* DONAL *visibly sags.* ARTIE *releases him.*

Look Donal . . .

DONAL (*waving away his words*). Do me a favour will yeh.

DONAL *leaves. Pause. Lights down. Lights rise on the belfry.* ARTIE *is sitting on the basket.* ANGELA *enters.*

ANGELA. How are yeh Artie?

ARTIE. Angela! Are yeh alright?

ANGELA. Yeah.

ARTIE. How are things at home?

ANGELA. You don't want to know.

ARTIE. Why, what did he say to yeh?

ANGELA. Ah I don't know . . . What didn't he say to me yeh mean! . . All hell broke loose on Tuesday night when he came home from work. Somebody wrote him a letter.

ARTIE. A letter? Who?

ANGELA. I don't know. I think it was the young fella.

ARTIE. What?

ANGELA. Donal wouldn't let me read it but I saw it in his hand. The writin' was all kind of scrawly and all.

ARTIE. Dominic?

ANGELA. Don't be too hard on him Artie. He loves you yeh know and I suppose he was afraid that he was goin' to lose you to me. So don't be too hard on him now will yeh?

ARTIE. What did he say in the letter?

ANGELA. He said that we were meetin' up here every night, that we were lockin' ourselves in and that. But sure poor Dominic probably didn't even realise the damage he was doin' like yeh know . . . I suppose I asked for it anyway didn't I?

ARTIE. What? . . . Yeah well maybe it's just as well now that it's all out in the open.

ANGELA. How do yeh mean?

ARTIE. I think we should go away somewhere together Angela for a while.

ANGELA. What? Look Artie I told yeh before I can't go away.

ARTIE. Why not? . . . Alright, so we stay here and face the music. We could live together. We're not the first Angela and we won't be the last either. I mean it happens like yeh know. Of course I'll have to get another job but sure . . .

ANGELA. Whoo Artie will yeh, slow down boy.

ARTIE. What?

ANGELA. It's over Artie. Finished.

ARTIE. What do yeh mean?

ANGELA. This is as far as we go. I thought you knew that?

ARTIE. Knew what? What are yeh talkin' about?

ANGELA. We got caught Artie and now it's over. I thought you understood that.

ARTIE. No I don't understand it. I mean to say I can't just turn all of this off like a tap yeh know.

ANGELA. Ah Artie don't give me a hard time now will yeh . . .

ARTIE. Look Angela . . .

ANGELA. Please Artie, don't.

ARTIE. Listen to me will yeh. Before you came along my life was dead. I was dead. You were the one who brought me back to life and I don't want it to end. I want it to last forever.

ANGELA. I know Artie but forever is a long, long time yeh know. A long, long time boy! Anyway by this time next year you'll be able to look back on all of this and . . .

ARTIE. This time next year! What are yeh talkin' about, this time next year. I mean what are yeh talkin' about?

ANGELA. Listen to me Artie, this is as far as we go. It's over now. Finished. I mean it . . . I'm sorry Artie. I never meant to hurt yeh or anythin' I swear. But this is as far as we can take it. I thought you knew that.

ARTIE. No I didn't know that.

He turns away. She goes to him.

ANGELA. . . . Here come on now. I brought you back to life and you taught me to soar again and that's somethin' isn't it? I soared in your arms Artie. The memory will last forever . . . I never said it was goin' to last Artie. I never said that.

DOMINIC *enters.*

DOMINIC. Can I watch yeh ringin' the bells Artie?

ARTIE. Not now Dominic. Later.

DOMINIC. What?

ARTIE. Look Dominic . . .

ANGELA. It's alright Artie, I've got to go now anyway . . . How are yeh Dominic?

DOMINIC. Angela.

She smiles at him. Pause.

ANGELA. I'll see yeh around Artie eh? . . .

ARTIE. Yeah, see yeh around.

Pause. ANGELA *leaves. Pause.*

DOMINIC. Are yeh alright Artie? What's wrong?

ARTIE. Why did yeh do it Dominic?

DOMINIC. What?

ARTIE. Why did yeh write the letter?

DOMINIC. What do yeh mean Artie?

ARTIE (*going angrily towards him*). Why did yeh do it?

DOMINIC (*backing away*). What?

ARTIE (*striking him*). Why did yeh do it? Why did yeh do it?

DOMINIC (*fleeing from the blows*). No Artie, no. Please Artie, no . . .

DOMINIC *falls down behind the basket.* ARTIE, *standing over him, takes off his belt and begins to whip the boy viciously with it.*

ARTIE. Why did yeh write the letter? Why did yeh do it? Why did
yeh do it . . .

DOMINIC. No Artie, no. I'm sorry Artie. I'm sorry. I'm terrible
sorry.

Lights down.

ACT TWO

Darkness. The sound of a bell ringing. Lights rise on the belfry. ARTIE *enters.*

ARTIE. Dominic! Dominic!

PAT (*emerging bleary-eyed from the shadows*). How are yeh Artie?

ARTIE. Pat! Is Dominic up here? I heard a bell ringin'.

PAT. That was me Artie. I rang it.

ARTIE. What?

PAT. I rang it. It was a sort of an S.O.S., Artie.

ARTIE. How do yeh mean?

PAT (*tearful*). I'm after breakin' out Artie. I'm drinkin' again. . . . I'm after lettin' everybody down, so I am.

ARTIE. I thought it was Dominic after runnin' away from the school again. Are yeh alright?

PAT. What? Yeah I'm O.K. I'm alright.

ARTIE. Do yeh want me to ring up Belmount for yeh or anythin'?

PAT. What? No, I can't go into Belmount now sure. I've too much to do. Sure I've the Confirmations and everythin' comin' up.

ARTIE. The Confirmations are not for another month Pat, so yeh needn't go usin' that as an excuse at all. Go into Belmount for a couple of weeks – get yourself sorted out. Here, give me the keys of your car. I'll ring up the hospital and let them know you're comin' and then I'll drop yeh down that far.

PAT. Tch . . . I've let everybody down again. I'm sorry Artie. I'm sorry.

ARTIE. Yeh haven't let anybody down at all – only yourself.

PAT. But sure I'm not cut out for this life Artie. It don't suit me at all boy. You don't understand that do yeh? I mean to say you can't what-do-you-call-it . . .

ARTIE. What's wrong with yeh now?

PAT. This is a queer lonely auld life Artie yeh know.

ARTIE. I know.

PAT. I've no friends or anythin'.

ARTIE. What are yeh talkin' about? You've lashin's of friends.

PAT. No. I've lashin's of aquaintances yeah. No friends though.
Thanks to this garb here. I mean to say Artie nobody talks
natural when I'm around in this get up. What am I'm talkin'
about I don't talk normal meself when I'm around. I'm like an
auld fella so I am. The things I come out with sometimes I'm not
coddin' yeh. Methuselah has nothin' on me I swear. Hello
Missus, how are all the care? . . . No I'm just not cut out for it
Artie. It don't suit me at all sure.

ARTIE. You're a good priest Pat. That's why people come and talk
to yeh all the time.

PAT. Huh! The blind leadin' the blind I think . . . I'm goin' to tell
yeh somethin' now Artie, just between you, me and the wall
there but sometimes I'm not too sure what it's all about any more
yeh know. I mean I don't . . . I mean I still believe and all the
rest of it. I always believe – but sometimes I don't know what it's
all about yeh know . . . I mean it's a queer auld lonely life boy.
Yeh know you're walkin' down a street and yeh see this lovely
woman gettin' out of a car or somethin' or a little family goin' by
on the other side of the road or yeh hear a crowd of young
people laughin' and singin' inside some public house. I'm tellin'
yeh Artie my heart sinks sometimes when I think of all the
things I'll never see and do and hear . . . I'm practically runnin'
this parish yeh know. Sure Father Matthews is bet.

ARTIE. Give us the keys Pat.

PAT. When I was a young student in the seminary I was sent out
to Rome one summer. I met this girl out there – knocked
around with her for the duration of my stay. Ah yeh should have
seen her Artie. She was like poetry in motion I'm not coddin'
yeh . . . The pair of us sittin' in the shade of an auld fountain or
skippin' up a side street away from the summer rain. The sound
of her dress swishin' against her legs when she walked. And her
laugh. Ah Jaysus Artie, yeh should have seen her laugh boy.
Poetry in motion I swear . . . Do you remember when I was an

altar boy here Artie? I fell in love with the place didn't I? The
smell of it! The whole atmosphere of it . . . I hate facin' all the
boys in the manse now.

ARTIE. No one 'll pay a blind bit of notice of yeh at all.

PAT. No, I suppose not. Sure people are very good alright aren't
they when yeh give them half a chance. People can be very kind.

He gives ARTIE *the keys.*

ARTIE. I'll meet yeh down in the vestry.

*ARTIE leaves. PAT breaks down and cries. Lights down. Lights rise.
ARTIE is standing downstage, facing the audience. In the background
we can see ANGELA and DOMINIC in the vestry. ANGELA is
washing out vases in the sink. DOMINIC is sitting on the chair
polishing two big candlesticks.*

ARTIE (*to the audience*). 'Sing us a song,' she said, 'on this day of
days.' This day of days! I've already told yeh how the day would
end. Now I suppose you'll need to know how it began . . . It
began with a glove. And a smile. And a woman singin' a sad, sad
song.

*ANGELA is singing 'Hi Lily Hi Low' as she works. DOMINIC seems
contented, soothed by the sound of her voice and by her presence. ARTIE
enters. ANGELA smiles at him.*

DOMINIC. What do yeh think of them Artie? Yeh can nearly see
your face in them boy. Auld Molly Delaney 'll be able to watch
her tonsils now while she's prayin'.

ARTIE hands ANGELA the glove.

ANGELA. Where did yeh find that? I was lookin' all over the place
for that.

DOMINIC. I found it inside there Angela. I was wantin' to run
after yeh with it but Artie wouldn't let me.

ANGELA. What? Have you been dressin' up again boy?

ARTIE. Yeah. It's not the same without the handbag though.

ANGELA chuckles.

DOMINIC. Did yeh know it's my birthday today Angela?

ANGELA. Is it hon? What age are yeh?

DOMINIC. I'm older than I look Angela and younger than I feel. Ain't that right Artie?

ARTIE. Yeah.

DOMINIC. I'm browned off doin' these boy.

ARTIE. Show. They're alright. They'll do. Go ahead out with them.

DOMINIC. What? Are they alright?

ARTIE. Yeah.

ANGELA. Where are they for Dominic, the transept?

DOMINIC. Yeah.

ANGELA. Well here, bring this vase out too when you're goin'.

DOMINIC. Oh here Angela what do yeh think I have, a hundred hands or somethin'?

ANGELA. Oh alright, sure you can come back for it.

DOMINIC. It's alright, give it to me . . . Hey Artie. Women!

DOMINIC *leaves.*

ANGELA. I'm not coddin' yeh he's after hintin' about a hundred times that it's his birthday, God help him. Listen I've a few things in the closet Artie for the party. You'd better bring them up because if he spots them we'll be all done for.

ARTIE. Right.

ANGELA *goes into the closet.*

ANGELA (*off*). Did you bring some stuff up already Artie yeah?

ARTIE. Yes I did.

ANGELA. What have yeh got?

ARTIE. I have all the drink up there and that. I got him a cake. A few sweets and biscuits and that kind of thing, yeh know. Ah we've lashin's of stuff for him.

ANGELA (*coming out, a few plates and things wrapped up in the tablecloth*). Yeah. I just made a plate of sandwiches, a few scones and a bit of a trifle. And I've a large bottle of lemonade here too. There's some paper plates and cups and a couple of paper hats and streamers and that. That's enough ain't it?

ARTIE. Lashin's. Sure there'll be only a handful of us in it anyway.

ANGELA. Well here you take them then and . . .

ARTIE. Hang on. I have an auld cardboard box here somewhere.

ANGELA. What? . . . Oh right! . . . (*She watches him fondly.*) Yeh know where everything is Artie, don't yeh?

ARTIE. Yeah. It's all organised. (ANGELA *chuckles.*)

DONAL *enters.*

DONAL. Did you want me Angela?

ANGELA. What? Oh yeah. I left Dominic's present at home Donal, I wonder could yeh bring it down to me?

DONAL. Yeah right. When are yeh wantin' it now? Because I've to go down to the alley.

ANGELA. What time are ye havin' it at Artie?

ARTIE. One o'clock. We have to wait for Father Pat yeh see. And Father Matthews might pop in too he said.

ANGELA. One o'clock, Donal. It won't go on too long Artie will it?

ARTIE. No. Sure we've the funeral at two.

ANGELA. And the weddin'.

ARTIE. Yeah, the weddin' at four.

DONAL. Busy people. Where is this yoke anyway Angela?

ANGELA. It's on the mantelpiece Donal. Yeh can't miss it. It's all wrapped up and all.

DONAL. Right. Listen have you any money on yeh?

ANGELA. Yeah, why?

DONAL. Give us a loan of a pound will yeh.

ANGELA. Tch . . . (*She goes to her bag.*)

DONAL. I'm just wantin' to buy an auld paper and that like, yeh know.

ANGELA. You're nothin' only a scourge boy, do yeh know that. Yes, a scourge yeh are! Here.

DONAL. I hope this is not your last pound now or anythin' is it?

ANGELA. I'm sure you're worried now.

DONAL (*putting his arm around her and drawing her towards him*). She loves me really though Artie yeh know. Don't yeh?

ANGELA (*fixing his tie*). Go ahead. And listen you make sure that you're back here by one and don't keep the young fella waitin' for his present, do yeh hear me?

DONAL (*kissing her*). Yeah right Bwana. Loud and clear. I'll see yeh Artie.

ARTIE. All the best.

DONAL *leaves*.

ANGELA. Never get married, Artie.

ANGELA *chuckles and goes back to the sink.* ARTIE *stands there watching her, the cardboard box in his hands. Lights down. Lights rise on the belfry. It is the closing stages of the birthday party.* DOMINIC *is sitting on a chair.* ANGELA *is tidying up.* FATHER PAT *is sitting on the basket.* DONAL *is standing over him.*

PAT. Oh they're a breed apart alright aren't they? Yes, a breed apart they are boy. But where would we be without them though, that's what I'd like to know. Sure we'd be lost wouldn't we?

DONAL. Yeah. God we would boy! . . . Yeh talk about women though lads. I was talkin' to poor auld Chas Whelan down in the pub the other night and he was tellin' us about this article that he was readin' in a magazine not too long ago and it was all about women – yeh know the mystique of them and all – their intuition and their what-do-you-call-it, their sexual allure and that. It was written by this doctor or professor or somethin' Chas was sayin'. He was some sort of an expert on women anyway, supposed to be. He reckoned that the idea that women were the weaker sex was a load of baloney. He went on to compare a woman to a beautiful sweet scented flower which could give off this aroma or whatever to enable her to attract all the males closer to her, yeh know. I can't remember now exactly how he put it but accordin' to Chas the general gist of the article anyway was that when they were all congregated around her, yeh know when they were all more or less under her spell, she'd just open up her mouth and swallow the whole feckin' lot of them. (*They laugh.*) It's a great comparison though ain't it?

ARTIE (*entering*). Are yeh alright lads?

PAT. Grand.

DONAL. Sound as a bell Artie. What time is it anyway? Ten to two. Jaysus I'd better be makin' tracks lads. Are you wantin' a lift over to the house or anythin' Artie?

ARTIE. No, I've work to do.

DONAL. Oh that's right, your man is gettin' buried today ain't he? What are you doin' hon?

ANGELA. I'll give Artie a hand here. Are you sayin' the weddin' mass, Father?

PAT. No, Father Matthews is sayin' it.

ANGELA. What about the funeral?

PAT. Father Matthews.

DONAL. You must be chargin' too much Father, are yeh? Either that or your man is under cuttin' yeh.

PAT. I must be doin' somethin' wrong alright Donal.

ARTIE. Poor Dominic is knackered there.

DONAL. What? Are yeh tired son?

DOMINIC. Yeah, I'm fairly tired alright.

ARTIE. Are yeh wantin' to go home or are yeh wantin' to do this funeral with me?

DOMINIC. What?

DONAL. Sure I'll run him home if he wants, Artie.

ARTIE. What are yeh wantin' to do Dominic?

DOMINIC. I'm wantin' to do the funeral with you.

ARTIE. Alright. Auld Molly Delaney sniffed us out anyway Dominic, didn't she? Hah?

DOMINIC. Yeah.

DONAL. She's well able to knock them back lads ain't she? She downed three or four bottles of stout there and it didn't take a feather off her boy. Yeh know, for a woman her age like.

ANGELA. Is she gone Artie, yeah?

ARTIE. Yeah, she's gone – staggerin' home.

DONAL. Yeah. She's gone down onto the quay to roll a couple of sailors Angela . . . Jaysus lads she has some tongue on her though hasn't she? I don't think I'd like a lash of it somehow or other would you? Hah?

ARTIE. Stop the noise, she'd fleece yeh that's all.

PAT. I'm goin' to tell yeh one thing lads, here and now for nothin', but whatever else they say about Molly Delaney she's a bloody good neighbour and one loyal friend so she is.

DONAL. I suppose.

ARTIE. Yeah. As the monkey said when he walked across the mirror, 'that's another way of lookin' at it.' *joke*

DONAL. What? (*He laughs.*)

ARTIE. Give us them keys there behind yeh Donal, will yeh.

DONAL. Yeah, right . . . There y'are Angela look, the keys of Saint Selskar in the palm of me hand. And they said it couldn't be done hah!

ARTIE. Thanks, Donal.

DOMINIC. So what?

DONAL. What?

DOMINIC. So what? as the sewin' machine said to the nudist. Do yeh get it?

DONAL. No.

DOMINIC. Sew what? Nothin' to sew! Do yeh get it?

DONAL. I think you're havin' me on boy are yeh? What?

DOMINIC. Go away from me will yeh.

DONAL. What? . . . Who told yeh that one?

DOMINIC. Artie, who do yeh think.

DONAL. That's a right one alright ain't it? Hah? Alright I'll ask you one now, right? Are yeh ready?

DOMINIC. Yeah.

DONAL. A man, a fox, a dog and a cat had to get to the other side of this river, right. But the man only had a small raft and so he could only take one of them at a time. How did he do it?

ANGELA (*from the steps*). Artie, yeh might give us up that auld box there will yeh.

ARTIE. Right.

DONAL. Bearin' in mind now that the dog 'll ate the cat and the fox 'll kill the dog if he leaves them alone together. How did he do it? The fox and the cat won't touch one another now.

DOMINIC. Well he brought the fox over first, right.

DONAL. Yeah and the dog 'll ate the cat on him!

DOMINIC. Oh yeah, I forgot about that.

ANGELA (*taking the box from* ARTIE). I love your arms Artie.

ARTIE. What's that?

ANGELA. I say you've lovely arms.

DOMINIC. He brought the dog over first though.

DONAL. Yeah.

DOMINIC. And then he went back and got the cat.

DONAL. Yeah and then what did he do?

DOMINIC. He went back to get the . . . Wait there now.

DONAL. Ah yeh see you're snookered now. Hah (*Laughs.*) He brings the dog over first, right. Then he goes back and gets the cat. But he brings the dog back with him and leaves him on the other side again while he brings over the fox. Then he goes back for the dog.

DOMINIC. Oh yeah.

PAT (*chuckling*). That's a good one Donal.

DONAL. What? (DONAL *looks at* PAT *and laughs.*)

DOMINIC. Alright I'll ask you one. What did the monkey say when he sat on the razor blade? And they're off! Do yeh get it? They're off! (*He laughs.*)

ARTIE. Yeh might give us that coat there behind yeh, Father will yeh.

PAT. Yeah, right. I'll go meself Artie I think. I'll see yeh Dominic. God bless yeh. Good luck Donal.

DONAL. Are yeh off, Father?

PAT. Yeah. I'll see yeh Angela. Thanks very much. Well done.

ANGELA (*off*). I'll see yeh, Father.

PAT. Goodbye lads. (*He leaves.*)

DONAL. Good luck Father.

DOMINIC. What did the money say when the train ran over his tail?

DONAL. Oh here let me out of here.

DOMINIC. It won't be long now. Do yeh get it? It won't be long now.

DONAL. I'll see yeh, Artie. Angela I'm off. I'll see yeh later on eh!

ANGELA (*off*). Right.

DOMINIC. What did the monkey say when he threw the clock out the window? (DONAL *exits.* DOMINIC *follows him.*) . . . Time flies!

They are gone and ARTIE *is left alone. He takes a letter from his pocket.*

ARTIE (*to the audience*). I found this up in the attic. It's a letter from me Da.

(*He reads.*)

Dear Kate,

I am writing to you in the hope that I might entice you and the boy to join me here in London. I have a fairly good job here now on the railway and the room that I am living in at the moment is spacious enough for all of us.

As you know I cannot return again to Wexford. Under the circumstances I would find it impossible to hold my head up in the town. I know it's been hard for you but it's been hard for me too. To have to stand on the sidelines and watch you and the boy slipping away has been heartbreaking for me. I don't want to come between you and your father but sooner or later you're going to have to decide one way or another. I mean to say I believe that your place is with me and mine with you, even if it is only for the boy's sake.

Please think carefully about all I have said and if you do decide to join me then I could send you the fare next week. We could make a new start here Kate and I'm sure between the two of us we could build a brand new life for ourselves. Please write soon. I've enclosed a five pound postal order.

Love,
Frankie.

P.S. Please excuse the writing. I have a bit of a blister on my thumb.

He looks down at the letter and sighs.

All my life yeh know, whenever I put a foot astray me poor Da used to get the blame for it. If I got into a fight at school or stayed out late or somethin'. The only time I ever heard her give him any credit was the night I was goin' off to my first dance. I was kind of nervous about it and she came across and straightened my tie and told me not to worry. She said that me Da used to be a great dancer in his day. 'He won medals and everythin' for it,' says she. Unfortunately I didn't follow in his footsteps that night. I stood down at the back of the hall all evenin', rooted to the spot. I was terrified to ask anyone up to dance. I was afraid of me life there was a smell of incense off of me to tell yeh the truth . . .

ANGELA *enters and begins rooting in the basket.*

ARTIE. Excuse the handwritin' says he. I wouldn't mind but it's as neat as a pin . . . Me mother wasn't exactly over the moon when I showed her this letter yeh know. She went into her act straight away about him. 'Oh for God's sake Ma,' says I to her. 'He was just an ordinary man.' He was a corner boy of the highest order,' says she, 'hangin' around bettin' shops and snooker halls and all the rest of it. And that's the man you're wantin' to meet, that's the hand you're dyin' to shake. Well away with yeh boy,' says she, 'because as far as I can see you're the very same as him at the back of it all . . .' And then I showed her the photograph and she went all quiet and her eyes filled up.

Slight pause.

ANGELA. The heart's its own boss Artie I think. People can give their love away as freely as they want but not the heart. The heart's its own boss boy!

ARTIE *puts the letter away.*

I have a photo at home yeh know that keeps turnin' up to kind of haunt me all the time. I'll find it in a drawer or somewhere or down in the end of my handbag when I'm rootin' around for my keys. No idea how it got there! . . . It was taken on the steps of White's Hotel. Donal's mother and father's fiftieth anniversary it was. We had a bit of a do for them. All the lads came home from England and all for it. This was supposed to be a picture of just the immediate family so I stepped back into the hotel doorway out of the way. It had been snowin' and the steps leadin' up to the hotel were still covered in slush. I think the photographer must have had a few drinks in him or somethin' because when it came out you could see me as clear as day standin' in the background. I looked like a little orphan standin' there in the cold. Everybody laughed when they saw it. It was as if I didn't belong in Donal's life at all. You'd swear I was tryin' to sneak my way into it or somethin'. Or out of it, whichever the case may be. It's a great photograph though. I'm not coddin' yeh, you can nearly hear them all laughin' in it . . .

She chuckles and goes behind the raised lid of the basket, out of sight.

Our Maude says that there's only two real choices open to people in life yeh know. Whether to tap the good side of them or the bad side. If yeh tap the good side then all you'll see is the good in people and the good in everything and you'll be happy. If yeh tap the bad side of yeh then you'll be devious and snakey and bad and you'll never be really contented. Everytime I look at that photograph I keep thinkin' how contented they all look and I keep wonderin' why I'm not in there with them . . . (*She emerges, wearing only an altar boy's surplus.*) Do yeh think I've tapped the bad side of me Artie?

ARTIE. No.

ANGELA. Huh? This is about the length of the dresses that meself and Maude used to wear now when we'd be goin' off to the dances. Me poor Da used to nearly do his nut. 'There's no point in havin' nice legs Daddy if you're not prepared to show them off,' we'd say to him. . . . What do yeh think?

ARTIE *goes to her and takes her in his arms.*

ARTIE. I want to kiss your heart. I want to climb inside yeh and kiss your heart.

ANGELA. Oh Artie, I soar in your arms I swear. Soar I do boy!

ARTIE. I want every minute I spend with you to last forever.

ANGELA. Careful Artie, forever is a long, long time yeh know. A long, long time boy!

Lights down. Lights rise to find ARTIE alone.

ARTIE (*to the audience*). That's what she said. Forever is a long, long time. And it is too. Without her anyway . . . I saw her last week at Dominic's funeral. There was a good crowd at it. It seems poor Dominic in his own simple way touched more people's lives than the whole lot of us put together. And now I keep thinkin' about the last time I saw him alive. He was after runnin' away from the school again, hitched a lift into Wexford. Naturally enough he came straight to the chapel. I rang up the school to let them know where he was and while we were waitin' for someone to come and get him I brought him up into the belfry out of harm's way.

Lights rise on the belfry. DOMINIC *is ringing the bell, dangling from the rope and swinging his legs wildly in the air and so on.*

DOMINIC. Did yeh ever see this one Artie?

ARTIE. What? Mind yeh don't hurt yourself now.

DOMINIC. What?

ARTIE. I said be careful.

DOMINIC. But sure this is nothin' Artie. Do yeh know little Kevin Bennett. He used to be an altar boy here one time. He was so light that he was able to climb up to the top of the rope without even ringin' the bell . . . And the Dumper McGrath used to swing from here over to there and he'd play the chimes with his feet boy. If you had known half the things that went on up here Artie you'd 've done your nut so yeh would.

ARTIE *chuckles to himself.*

ARTIE. So what do yeh think of the school then?

DOMINIC. It's alright.

ARTIE. Do yeh like it though?

DOMINIC. No, I hates it.

ARTIE. Well are yeh learnin' anythin' up there?

DOMINIC. Yeah, I'm learnin' to make chairs. I've a pain in me face makin' 'em to tell yeh the truth. Thousands of them. I hates 'em.

ARTIE. Yeh know Dominic there's only two things I can't stand in life, boy.

DOMINIC. What's that?

ARTIE. A one-legged man and a three-legged chair.

DOMINIC *laughs half-heartedly.*

DOMINIC. Sure that's nothin' Artie, a fella in our class had a brainwave last week. He told the teacher that we should start makin' five-legged chairs for big fat people – people with big arses and all. It'd be queer good though wouldn't it? Hah?

ARTIE. Yeah.

DOMINIC *whistles softly through his teeth.*

DOMINIC. Our teacher is half blind yeh know . . . Love tail dove tail, the tail of a dove . . . You should get a different job Artie.

ARTIE. What?

DOMINIC. You should get a different job. You should get a job makin' people happy. That'd be a right job wouldn't it?

ARTIE. Yeah.

DOMINIC. We were all brought down to this big hotel last week from the school Artie and there was this fella up on the stage with a microphone in his hand. My job here today, says he, is to make you people happy. That's exactly what he said boy.

ARTIE. Aye? And did he?

DOMINIC. Yeah. He made me happy anyway. That's what I'm wantin' to be when I grow up Artie. I'm wantin' to make people happy.

ARTIE. How are yeh goin' to do that Dominic?

DOMINIC. Easy. I'll get them all in a big room, right. And I'll say to them, 'My job is to make you people happy. What do yez want?' And when they tell me what they want I'll give it to them and I'll say to them, 'Now are yez happy?' And when they say yes I'll give them all what they want again. I'll do that about ten times boy. I'm not coddin' yeh I'll sicken them all so I will. They'll never want to be happy again. (*He laughs.*) That's a right one Artie ain't it, hah? . . . Spwead some jam on my bwead said Fwed.

ARTIE. Tell us Dominic, how are yeh gettin' on up there though really? I mean do yeh miss your Aunt and Uncle now or anythin'?

DOMINIC. Yeah. I miss them alright Artie. And will I tell yeh what else I miss? Do yeh want to know? Chips! They'd hardly ever give yeh chips boy. I swear. Yeh think yeh were askin' for the moon or somethin' . . . Oh by the way Artie I have somethin'

for you too . . . (*He takes out a key*.) Do yeh know what this is
Artie. The spare key to the belfry. Little Kevin Bennett and the
Dumper McGrath were ragin' when you gave this to me yeh
know. 'Go away,' says the Dumper to me one day, 'with your
rusty auld key to nowhere.' But what he didn't know Artie was
that this is the key to the Catacombs too. I bet yeh you didn't
even know that Artie did yeh? I brought the two of them down
there one time and I locked them in. 'Who has a rusty auld key
to nowhere now,' says I to them. The pair of them were afraid of
their shit of the dark boy! . . . I used to take this with me
everywhere I went yeh know Artie. I'd change it out of one
pocket and into another whenever I'd be goin' anywhere. And
do yeh want to know why Artie? Because no matter where I was
– at the pictures or down in Bryne's Cafe or maybe over in the
auld handball alley or somewhere – I always knew that I was the
only one there who had a key to the belfry. The only one Artie!
And then when I'd be goin' home in the dark after I'd take it
out and I'd scrape it against the wall and I'd run along with it
until the sparks came flyin' out behind me. And do yeh want to
know what it was like, Artie? It was like being in the bumpers in
the carnival, that's what it was like boy. The time I saw me Aunty
and me Uncle goin' in the bumpers and I got a bit of a fright
when I saw all the sparks comin' out of the ceilin'. I started
shoutin' at them and everythin'. 'The sky's on fire,' says I but
sure nobody could hardly hear me over all the noise and all. I
thought the sky was on fire. (*He chuckles*.) They never even
invited me to the weddin' nor nothin' boy! . . . You'd want to
hang on to this now Artie because if anything ever happens to
your key you'll need this one to get in here won't yeh? Hah?
(ARTIE *takes the key from him*.) Spwead some jam on my bwead
said Fwed I'll tell yeh one thing Artie, you're alright! . . . (*Pause*.)

FATHER PAT *enters*.

PAT. They're down there Artie.

ARTIE. Oh are they? Right.

PAT. How are yeh, Dominic?

DOMINIC. How are yeh, Father. You'll be glad to know Father
that I never went near the chimes.

PAT. Good lad.

ARTIE. This fella was tellin' me Father that he's learnin' to make
chairs up there.

PAT. Aye?

ARTIE. Yeah.

DOMINIC. I've a pain in me face makin' 'em Father.

PAT. Who's teachin' yeh to make 'em?

DOMINIC. Mister 'Burn the house' Murphy.

PAT. Why do yeh call him that?

DOMINIC. Because he burnt his Ma's house down to get the insurance money that's why.

PAT. Do yeh like him?

DOMINIC. No, I hates him. There's two things I can't stand Father. Three things though. Do yeh know what they are?

PAT. No, what?

DOMINIC. Love tail, dove tail and the tail of a dove. Hey Artie, did your Ma die?

ARTIE. Yeah.

DOMINIC. When did she die?

ARTIE. A couple of weeks ago.

DOMINIC. Did she? . . . She was one contrary woman Father. Wasn't she Artie? The shouts and bawls of her up in the bed boy. Stop the noise, Father. The roars of her, says Artie, and the bawls of him. Remember the day I ate the grapes on her Artie. She nearly had a fit didn't she? I wouldn't mind but she wasn't goin' to ate them herself anyway. Yeh should have seen her in the bed Father, a great big dressin' gown on her and all. King Coitus Interruptus the Second had nothin' on her boy!

PAT. What did he say?

ARTIE. Are you wantin' to play a hymn before yeh go boy?

DOMINIC. What? Yeah, alright.

PAT. I'll go down and tell them you're comin' Artie.

ARTIE. Yeah right Pat. Thanks.

  PAT *leaves*.

ARTIE. What one are yeh goin' to play?

DOMINIC. I don't know. Not that one there anyway.
(*Satisfaction.*) . . . Love tail, dove tail, 'Sweet Sacrament Divine'!

ARTIE. Right. Go on then.

> DOMINIC *plays the hymn which he knows by heart.* ARTIE *watches him proudly. Lights down. Lights rise.* ARTIE *is alone in the belfry.*

ARTIE (*to the audience*). Me mother never got over the operation. She lingered in hospital for a few days and then one night she just passed away peacefully in her sleep. We buried her on a cold dismal day. It was a small funeral. The next couple of weeks were terrible for me. I felt as if there was a big black cloud hangin' over me, bearin' down on me all the time. I'd go back to my little empty house and everywhere I'd turn I'd find somethin' to remind me of her. I felt so lonely, I swear I'd just want to curl up and die. Then one day I caught a glimpse of Angela goin' down the street in front of me and all of a sudden the whole thing just sort of lifted. All of a sudden I was my father's son again. I slipped into a bettin' shop to get away from the rain and while I was waitin' I put a couple of quid on a horse called Baby Blue. It came in at eight to one. So I went home and I got all dressed up and that night I went out on the town. I went into a lounge bar to hear The Ferrymen. I had a right night. Later on I rambled into a late night snooker hall and the whole place turned to look at me. After a few months though they'd be steppin' back out of my way. I'm not coddin' yeh the snooker cue just seemed to belong in my hand. A pack of cards the very same. I've always been blessed with a good memory and I'm goin' to tell yeh one thing but it didn't take me too long to fleece a couple of fellas who would have considered themselves sharks. One fella – Shepherd Kelly – was a bad loser and he reared up on me one night. I've since discovered of course that all good players are bad losers, includin' me. Anyway this fella tossed the deck of cards into my face and called me a jamie bastard and I surprised everyone when I stretched him across the table with a box in the jaw. Oh yes, a hidden reservoir she tapped . . . I bought a tombstone for my mother's grave and a load of those sparkly stones. It looks nice now. I go out there every Sunday to say a few prayers for her. I hope I won't have a small funeral. It's nice over there on the other side of the river though. You can taste the tang of the sea and the seaweed and that and all the other little wild things that can't be caught or what-do-you-call-it . . . tamed. It's kind of wild over there like yeh know . . . It's nice though!

DONAL *enters*.

DONAL. How are yeh, Artie?

ARTIE. Donal!

DONAL. I was down in the vestry lookin' for yeh. Someone told me that you were up here.

ARTIE. Oh right.

DONAL. Jaysus that was rough about the young fella wasn't it?

ARTIE. Yeah.

DONAL. He was runnin' away from the school or somethin' wasn't he?

ARTIE. Yeah. The poor little divil ran right out under a car. Killed outright.

DONAL. Tch . . . Ah well that's somethin' I suppose.

ARTIE. How are all your lads?

DONAL. Grand.

ARTIE. I see young Marty Murray did fairly well out in Toronto after anyway.

DONAL. Yeah. He won all before him out there by all accounts. Fair play to him! . . . Listen Artie, yeh haven't seen Angela lately or anythin' have yeh?

ARTIE. Angela? No. I caught a glimpse of her at Dominic's funeral alright but I haven't been talkin' to her lately or anything like yeh know. Why?

DONAL. Ah I was just wonderin . . . (*He goes to the window.*) Yeh can nearly see half the town from here. Poor auld Chas Whelan with the big ladders on his bike. He's supposed to be doin' my roof. And all the auld dog sheds and pigeon lofts at the back of the people's houses hah! A Town Without Pity! Did yeh ever see that picture Artie? Kirk Douglas. It was good . . .

Pause.

DONAL. I've a feelin' Angela is at it again Artie.

ARTIE. What?

DONAL. She's seein' someone else I think.

ARTIE. How do yeh know?

DONAL. The usual signs . . . Yeah, I know, why do I stay with her. A good question! . . . Yeh know when I was out in Toronto a few years ago there was a woman out there who took a great shine to me. She was all over me I swear. I'd say I could have had anythin' I wanted off of her boy. And no one would have been any the wiser either . . . But I didn't. I couldn't . . . (*He touches the rope.*) Your auld job now Artie is to keep on ringin' this big bell here. Mine is to make sure that Angela has somewhere to come home to. Because sooner or later she's goin' to get hurt more than the whole lot of us put together yeh know.

Pause.

ARTIE. Donal, do yeh remember the letter that yeh got that time.

DONAL. Yeah. Why, what about it?

ARTIE. Well I was often wonderin' about it like yeh know.

Pause. DONAL *takes out his wallet and takes from it the crumpled letter. He hands it to* ARTIE.

DONAL. Here, take it. Keep it. It's like a dagger through my heart anyway every time I look at it.

DONAL *leaves.* ARTIE *reads the letter.*

ARTIE (*to the audience*). It was me mother who wrote the letter not Dominic. Me mother! Thanks to Molly Delaney. The spy who came in from the cauld hah! . . . Poor Dominic! . . . Oh I never told yeh did I? I slept with a woman since. In a bed! A young widow called Rita. I met her at the Bacon Factory Reunion. I've been seein' her on and off for the past couple of months now. To tell yeh the truth the first time we didn't actually do anything. She cried a little bit and I sort of cried a little bit and then we fell asleep . . . I mean to say it's not what-do-you-call-it or anything – explosive! But it's alright like yeh know. It's nice. I like her anyway . . . Who knows hah? . . .

Lights down. Lights rise on the vestry. FATHER PAT *is knee-bent over a box of liturgical leaflets.*

PAT. I think we've enough of them Artie. There's three full boxes of them here sure.

ARTIE (*emerging from the closet*). What's that?

PAT. I say we hardly need any more of them. There's three full boxes of them here look. And as far as I know there should be another few of them inside there I think.

ARTIE. Oh yes there is. There's three or four more inside there, sure.

PAT. See what's in there will yeh. I'd say we've enough of them anyway.

ARTIE *goes into the closet.* ANGELA *enters.*

PAT. Hello Angela.

ANGELA. Hello Father.

PAT. How are yeh keepin'?

ANGELA. Grand.

PAT. And how's all the family?

ANGELA. Right form.

PAT. And Donal?

ANGELA. Good.

PAT. No fear of him, says you.

ANGELA. No. You're lookin' well yourself.

PAT. Draggin' the bull by the tail as they say Angela.

ANGELA. How are yeh all managin' here now?

PAT. To tell yeh the truth Angela the place is gone to the dogs since you left us so it has.

ANGELA. Is it? I'm sorry I had to leave in such a hurry Father but I was under a bit of pressure at home like, yeh know.

PAT. Oh sure, I know that Angela. You're right too. Your home and family comes first.

ANGELA. The altar looks nice.

PAT. Yeah. Poor Artie does his best.

ARTIE (*entering*). Yeah we've enough. There's six of 'em in there.

PAT. Look who's come to brighten up the place for us, Artie!

ANGELA. How are yeh, Artie?

ARTIE. Angela!

PAT. I was just tellin' her here Artie that the place is gone to the dogs since she left us ain't it?

ARTIE. Yeah, it surely is.

ANGELA. I was sorry to hear about your mother, Artie.

ARTIE. Thanks Angela.

ANGELA. And poor Dominic.

ARTIE. Yeah.

PAT. The poor crator anyway. I'm goin' to tell yeh one thing Angela but yeh'd miss him around the place here, wouldn't yeh Artie? Spwead some jam on my bwead said Fwed . . . The things he used to come out with sometimes. Of course this fella here used to encourage him. Do yeh remember the day he climbed out onto the chapel roof, Artie. I'm not coddin' yeh Angela but I nearly had heart failure when I went out and saw him runnin' along the roof and he wavin' down to meself and Molly Delaney. I mean to say if he had fallen off of that that day . . . God, he was an awful case.

PAT *bends to pick up the cardboard boxes of leaflets.*

ANGELA. I see you've been keepin' busy anyway Artie?

ARTIE. How do yeh mean?

ANGELA. I see your picture in the paper last week.

ARTIE. Oh yeah, the auld snooker tournament.

ANGELA. I never knew you placed snooker.

ARTIE. Ah I only took it up a few months ago like yeh know.

ANGELA. Yeh must be fairly handy at it to get into the semi final.

ARTIE. Yeah, I'm startin' to get the hang of it now alright.

PAT (*going towards the closet*). He's a bit of a dark horse I think Angela. . . . Yes a dark horse he is boy . . .

ARTIE. But sure by right I should never have entered that tournament in the first place.

PAT (*exiting*). I don't know!

ANGELA. Yeh have to take a few chances now and again Artie don't yeh . . . (*Pause.*) How are yeh anyway?

ARTIE. Alright. And yourself?

ANGELA. O.K. I heard you're courtin' strong this weather is that right?

ARTIE. Who was tellin' yeh that?

ANGELA. Oh I have my spies . . . Poor Rita. I went to school with her yeh know. She's a nice woman, Rita.

ARTIE. Yeah, she's a nice woman alright . . .

ANGELA. Mmn.

ARTIE. Donal came to see me a little while back there Angela.

ANGELA. Did he?

ARTIE. Yeah. He thinks that you're seein' somebody else. I think he thought it might be me again.

ANGELA *thinks about it and sighs. Pause.*

ARTIE. Oh I found out where me Da is after.

ANGELA. Yeah?

ARTIE. He's in Bristol, livin' in a sort of a hostel over there he is. I was talkin' to him the other day on the telephone. I think that woman was right about him, yeh know. He does have a deadly smile. I'm not coddin' yeh, yeh could sort of hear it in the sound of his voice yeh know. He nearly burst a blood vessel laughin' when he heard that I was the sacristan here. He's been married twice he was tellin' me. Once to a coloured woman from Cardiff. The second time to this older one that he met while he was workin' on the railway. He said he divorced the first one and the second one died laughin'. I think me mother was right to keep well away from him somehow or other. He's a bit of a boyo alright I'd say. I'm goin' to go over and see him as soon as I get me holidays here.

ANGELA. That's good Artie. I'm glad. So everything is alright then?

ARTIE. Yeah, everything's alright. I come in here every day. I go up to the belfry and ring the bells. I do me work and the sun shines.

ARTIE *shrugs.*

PAT (*entering*). Artie, yeh might get us out the petty-cash box there will yeh.

ARTIE. What? Yeah, right.

PAT. There's two things I can't stand in life Father, says the bould Dominic to me as he was gettin' into the car the last time I saw him. What's that, says I. A one-legged man, says he, and a three-legged chair. (*They all chuckle sadly.*) Sure God be good to him, he's in Heaven now.

ANGELA. Yeah . . . I'll go lads and leave yez in peace.

PAT. Are yeh off, Angela?

ANGELA. Yeah. I'll go out to the chapel Father and say a few prayers I think.

PAT. Good girl. Say one for me while you're out there, will yeh.

ANGELA. Right. I'll see yeh, Artie.

ARTIE. Yeah. Goodbye Angela.

She leaves. ARTIE *watches the empty doorway.* PAT *suddenly understands.*

How much are yeh wantin' out of this thing?

PAT. A couple of quid 'll do me.

ARTIE. What's this for now exactly?

PAT. I'm wantin' to buy meself a packet of fags . . . No, it's for soap inside there . . . It's for soap!

ARTIE. Do yeh know what boy but you're a royal headache sometimes so yeh are. Here.

PAT *laughs as* ARTIE *gives him the money.* ARTIE *puts the petty-cash box away.* PAT *gazes down at him sympathetically.* PAT *leaves. Lights down.*

Afterword

Easter 1986 – just two months after my first novel, *Tumbling Down*, has been published – and my first stage play, *The Boker Poker Club*, is packing them in at the Wexford Arts Centre. It is a community production with a strong local cast. I myself am playing Stapler the over-the-hill boxer. The lead part of Jimmy Brady, the small town tearaway, is played by a young Wexford actor called Gary Lydon who performs with such raw-boned intensity that he actually stuns the audience into silence every night.

Nine months later he would be propelled into the professional arena, playing the same part in the Bush Theatre in London and because of a slight casting problem, I too would get another chance to play Stapler for four performances. The play would then of course be retitled *A Handful of Stars*, and would have, I am happy to report, a successful run at the Bush.

What it was that pleased an English audience I'll never really know. And what stunned the Wexford audience into silence I can only guess. Perhaps in our hearts we all believe that we actually owe a little debt of gratitude to the small town rebel who refuses to have his wings clipped or his tongue tied, who refuses to swallow the bitter pill of convention or to accept the so-called rules and regulations that are applied within the seedy world of the snooker hall. Maybe we feel privileged to stand in his dangerous shadow and we long to walk a little bit of the way with him as he goes hurtling towards his own self destruction.

To understand how and why I came to write this play in the first place you'll need to bear in mind that I grew up in a small Irish town in the late fifties and early sixties, a great cinematic era. We had three cinemas in our town at that time, and each cinema showed two houses each night, with a change of programme every second night, and I would try and see every picture that came to town. *A Handful of Stars* is dedicated to that era. It is a tribute to *Killer Dino* and *Rebel Without a Cause*, to *Cool Hand Luke* and to *The Last Picture Show*. To all the cowboy pictures and war stories I've seen. To Brando and Dean, Newman, Clift and McQueen. To all the young rebels who unknowingly sacrificed themselves so that the rest of us could be set free.

After *A Handful of Stars* the Bush commissioned me to write a second play for them. There was no talk of a trilogy yet. I began work on a play called *Runaway*, which told the story of Johnny Doran, a sullen young man who refused to wrap himself up in the flag of his tribe. It was set on the day of the All Ireland Hurling Final, and when more than half the town went off to Dublin to cheer for their own home team Johnny stayed brooding behind on the deserted streets to pour buckets of silent scorn on the bonfires that would soon be raging all around him. In the end he cleared off with a carnival, leaving in his wake a trail of broken hearts.

But when the Bush got around to reading the first draft they hinted that perhaps they had seen this character before – in Jimmy Brady from my previous play. I argued that there was more than one kind of small town rebel, that Johnny Doran did not possess the charm of Jimmy Brady and was therefore a darker and more evil character. The Bush stood their ground and in the end I acquiesced, secretly relishing the chance to burst the play wide open anyway. And so *Poor Beast in the Rain* was born – a rainy day sort of a play which is held together by an ancient Irish Myth as Danger Doyle returns like Oisín to the place of his birth, 'just because he wanted to see his auld mates again'. Danger Doyle, who is a sort of grown up Jimmy Brady, ran away with another man's wife ten years ago and the play is really about all the people the pair of them left behind.

It was during the writing of *Poor Beast in the Rain*, that the idea of a third play came to me. It was supposed to be set in a barber shop, telling the story of a small town barber who was a likeable rogue. The story would be told by a lonely little sacristan who loved and admired the barber. But when it came time for him to speak he decided in his wisdom not to go next or near the barber shop. In fact he refused to even mention the barber. He had his own story to tell. 'I know what they think of him', he began and the rest is history now.

In the first draft the mother was actually an on-stage character, haranguing poor Artie from her elevated bed. But during the first meeting with the Bush to discuss all the ins and outs of the play Robin Lefevre, the director, expressed a few qualms that he had about it all. He wasn't sure about the title, *Belfry*. 'I mean to say', he said, 'if it was set in a room you wouldn't call it *Room*, would you?' 'Also', he said, 'I have a real problem with the mother.' 'Would you like me to sack her?' I asked. 'Yes', he replied. 'Sack the mother.'

Now this sentence, 'Sack the mother', should go down in theatrical history as the most concise and unpretentious piece of advice that any director can dole out to a writer in his hour of need. It sure beats the lard out of the usual gobbledegook that we have to listen to.

Regarding the title: I went through the next few months racking my brains for a new title, coming up with all sorts of flowery and embarrassing names only for Robin to turn around two months later and ask, 'Well what was wrong with *Belfry*, anyway?' 'Exactly! Sack the mother and shoot the director', says I.

Finally in having to re-read the three plays again and to re-assess the work, I would like to put this one last notion to you and that is that the chasm between Jimmy Brady and Artie O'Leary is not as great as we have all come to fear. I mean to say Jimmy Brady could never be an Artie O'Leary, but there is a chance that Artie could have been a Jimmy Brady and that's good news for all of us because it means that the gap between us and the McQueens and the Brandos of this world is at least assailable. So in the words of Tennessee Ernie Ford, 'If you see me coming, better step aside. A lot of men didn't and a lot of men died . . .'

Billy Roche.
December 1991.

BILLY ROCHE

Billy Roche was born in Wexford where he now lives with his wife Patty and their three daughters. His first novel, *Tumbling Down* was published in 1986 by Wolfhound Press. He has written three plays to date, known collectively as *The Wexford Trilogy*. They are *A Handful of Stars* which won the John Whiting Award and the Plays and Players Award for the Most Promising Playwright, *Poor Beast in the Rain* which won the Thames TV Bursary Award, the Charrington Fringe Award and the George Devine Award, and thirdly *Belfry*. All three plays were first performed at The Bush Theatre, London. He is currently under commission with both the Royal Shakespeare Company and The Royal Court. In 1989 he was the writer in residence at the Bush Theatre.

As an actor Billy has played Stapler the boxer in *A Handful of Stars* at the Bush, Willie Diver in Brian Friel's *Aristocrats* at the Hampstead Theatre and Joe in *Poor Beast in the Rain* at Andrew's Lane Theatre, Dublin. He played a small part in David Hare's film, *Strapless* and his television work includes *The Bill*.

He has just recently finished his second novel which is called *The Sound of a Lonely Note*.